IT'S A GOOD DAY TO CHANGE THE WORLD

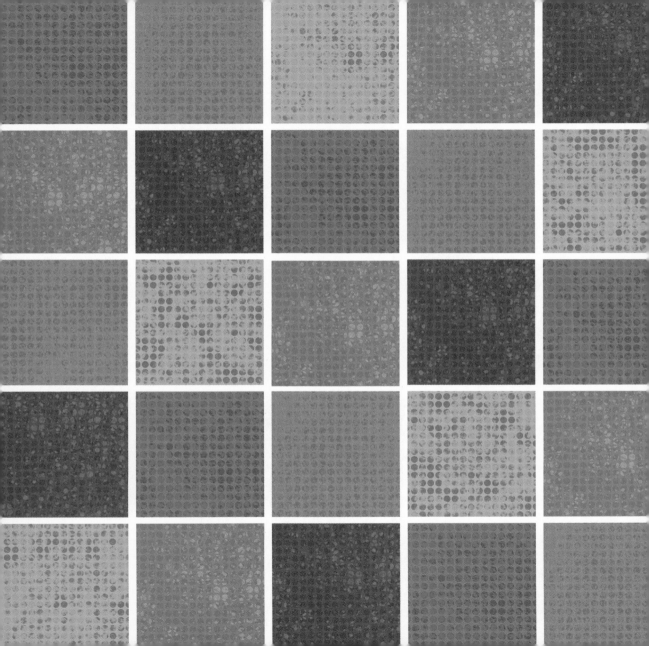

IT'S A GOOD DAY TO CHANGE THE WORLD

INSPIRATION AND ADVICE FOR A FEMINIST FUTURE

Countryman Press

An Imprint of W. W. Norton & Company
Celebrating a Century of Independent Publishing

LAUREN SCHILLER & HADLEY DYNAK
ILLUSTRATIONS BY ROSY PETRI

For information about permission to reproduce selections from this book, write to
Permissions, Countryman Press, 500 Fifth Avenue, New York, NY 10110

For information about special discounts for bulk purchases, please contact
W. W. Norton Special Sales at specialsales@wwnorton.com or 800-233-4830

Manufacturing by Versa Press
Book design by Allison Chi
Production manager: Devon Zahn

Countryman Press
www.countrymanpress.com

An imprint of W. W. Norton & Company, Inc.
500 Fifth Avenue, New York, NY 10110
www.wwnorton.com

978-1-68268-788-8

10 9 8 7 6 5 4 3 2 1

To our daughters, our mothers, our fathers, our brothers,
our husbands, and the many other feminists in our lives.
You keep us going.

"Everyone was so shocked and panicky.
No one knew what was ahead."
—Dorothea Lange

"These periods of chaos are cyclical.
I sense we're on an upward spiral."
—Betty Reid Soskin

CONTENTS

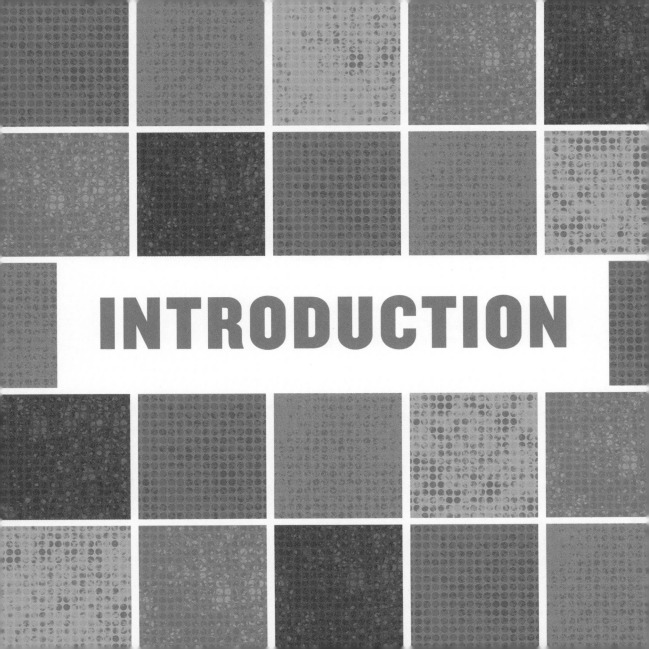

INTRODUCTION

The world we want is equal, just, and full of joy. A sustainable world that celebrates and elevates diverse perspectives, backgrounds, and abilities. One that rejects hate, violence, and discrimination, and moves away from outdated thinking about gender and gender roles. An equitable and inclusive society where we care about each other, listen to each other, and trust each other. So what does it take to achieve this vision when every day seems to bring new attacks on progress—and how do we sustain ourselves when the work is daunting?

To answer this question we bring you the stories of thirty trailblazers leading change right now.

IT'S A GOOD DAY TO CHANGE THE WORLD

We wrote this book because America is in the midst of cultural, environmental, and political turmoil. Yet, we believe in a feminist future where everyone can thrive. Every day, actions large and small can help us get there together.

We're Lauren and Hadley, the team behind *Inflection Point with Lauren Schiller,* an award-winning, nationally syndicated radio show and podcast about how women rise up, build power, and lead change. Founded in 2015 on KALW Public Media in San Francisco, the show was among the first to document the progress of women during a particularly profound moment in history. Despite constant chaos, oppressive discourse, and pervasive societal challenges, *Inflection Point* guests stepped up time and again to claim leadership roles, raise their voices, and protect our fundamental rights.

More than 200 activists, artists, authors, academics, entrepreneurs, and visionaries have appeared on the show. In every recording, they shared their remarkable achievements and spoke candidly about the hurdles they faced. The uniquely intimate space Lauren created made it possible to have honest and heartfelt conversations about the most pressing issues of our time. The result is a rich resource of inspiration, advice, and encouragement. We'll show you what we learned—and how you can blaze trails too.

WHO'S IN THIS BOOK

In this book, we've included thirty of these stories, edited and condensed to capture key lessons and moments of insight. We aimed to cover not only a wide variety of issues but also points of view that made us question our own biases and reconsider things we'd taken for granted. You'll find women you may know well and discover others you may be meeting for the first time. They are fighting for women's rights, reproductive justice, climate justice, food justice, common sense gun laws, disability rights, and LGBTQ+ rights. They are pushing back against racism, sexism, and sexual assault and harassment. They are building women's political power, demanding equity in caregiving, and making invisible problems visible. And they are creating art and media that redefine cultural norms and reimagine broken systems.

The people in this book come from a range of ages, geographies, cultural backgrounds, and identities. They can't represent everyone working for equality, but they all illustrate the possibilities for change.

Among them are Favianna Rodriguez, who uses art and activism to shift hearts and minds; Joan Blades, who pushes us to rebuild respectful relationships across party lines; Gloria Steinem, who encourages us to do something outrageous in the name of social justice; writer Ijeoma Oluo, who asks us to question our own privilege; journalist Rebecca Traister, who shares the transformational value of anger; and environmental leader Heather McTeer Toney, who guides us to empower the next generation.

A GUIDEBOOK FOR CHANGE

Each one of these stories is powerful. When we looked at them as a collection, a clear pattern emerged. One that revealed an essential guide for action with five steps for change:

1. IMAGINE—Dream of a New Way
2. PREPARE—Assemble Your Resources and Summon Your Bravery
3. CREATE—Put It All Together
4. TRANSFORM—Catalyze Change
5. SHARE—Celebrate, Gather, and Grow

Each chapter focuses on one step and features six inspiring stories paired with practical "Tools to Change the World" and "Advice to Keep Going."

You'll learn how to get outside your comfort zone, turn outrage into action, shift the cultural narrative, and share your truth. You'll discover what it takes to push new ideas forward, calculate risks, put pressure on those who hold power, and much more.

You'll also find examples of how to sustain yourself along the way. Making change is exhilarating, but it's also exhausting. To keep going, we must take care of ourselves and each other. For some this may mean taking time to nurture a plant or connect with a loved one. For others it may mean turning off devices, tuning in to new ideas, or finding ways to grapple with hard truths you encounter in our world every day.

Change doesn't always happen in a straight line. It is often an iterative process, a virtuous circle, or an "upward spiral," to quote Betty Reid Soskin (who appears in the Share Chapter, page 187). It's our intention that the steps, tools, and advice we've included will apply to any issue you face, whenever you face it, and wherever you are in your change-making journey.

A VISUAL METAPHOR

Artist Rosy Petri's stunning illustrations capture the vibrancy and energy of each profile. The textures, layers, and lines in every piece demonstrate that we are each unique and yet also made up of the same parts. The vivid color palette distinguishes each step, simultaneously providing contrast and areas of overlap. When viewed together, these artworks offer a beautiful representation of our collective impact.

OUR HOPE FOR YOU

Whether you want to tackle global issues or those in your own neighborhood; whether you want to reconfigure an entire system or connect with a person who has a different perspective; and whether or not you call yourself a feminist, are a friend of a feminist, or just want to live in a more equal world, this guide is for you.

It's a Good Day to Change the World is our small contribution to the larger effort to shake up the status quo. We hope you will find what you need in these pages to rise up and make change today, then do it again tomorrow.

These trailblazers inspired us to write this book. What will they inspire in you?

—LAUREN AND HADLEY

"

Making change is exhilarating, but it's also exhausting. In order to keep going, we must take care of ourselves and each other.

"

IMAGINE

DREAM OF A NEW WAY

The first step toward change is to dream with ambition. Maybe it's a flash of insight or maybe it's something you've imagined for a long time. Our dreams are kernels of the past and hopes for the future. They are possibilities born from claiming our power. So dream big. And remember that small ideas are sometimes the most revolutionary.

The visionary leaders in this chapter are clear about the world they want to live in. They push big ideas forward, shift culture, and rewrite old rules. They lead with kindness and try not to "give an F" about what others may think. They don't give up. And to sustain themselves they emphasize personal growth—by caring for living things, reading history, making art, and journaling about their experiences.

FAVIANNA RODRIGUEZ

IMAGINE IF WE ALL BELONGED

We all deserve to feel valued and heard in our daily interactions, and to see ourselves reflected in the culture around us. Music, movies, images, and stories can perpetuate the status quo, or they can open minds to a new normal. Favianna Rodriguez is a first-generation American Latinx artist and activist. She is also the cofounder and president of The Center for Cultural Power, a nonprofit that supports artists to accelerate social change through their work. In her visual art, public art, and writing, she focuses on migration, gender justice, climate change, racial equity, and sexual freedom. When she first spoke publicly about having an abortion, she upended social and cultural norms, and opened up a path for others to do the same.

"

If we can change culture, we can change people's imaginations.

"

FAVIANNA'S STORY

"I grew up in Oakland when it was one of the most dangerous cities to live during the era of crack cocaine. My parents just wanted me to get straight A's and an education. They were both holding down two to three jobs, and they didn't have a high school or college education, so education was a way for me to find my power. Their message was, 'Go to school, get straight A's. That's why we came to this country. And keep your legs closed!'

I got pregnant in my third year of college. When I told my partner at the time, he disappeared and I didn't see him again. So I was alone. It was thanks to Planned Parenthood that I was able to get an abortion, but it took me ten years to come out of the closet with my journey.

As a woman of color, I've always grown up around powerful women of color, but the narratives around control of our bodies are still so highly stigmatized. I was one of the first Latinas to publicly share their abortion story, and *Cosmo for Latinas* actually covered it. I talked about the power it takes for us to share our histories and to shed the shame. It's not just about abortion, it's fundamentally about the freedom to live our fullest selves in our bodies, tap into our joy, and make decisions about our bodies as we see fit."

TOOLS TO CHANGE THE WORLD

Understand who is driving popular culture

"I was always very aware growing up in the '80s, watching movies like *Sixteen Candles* and *Pretty in Pink,* that there was no consent. A lot of the culture projected back to us—whether it's music or film or even the ads we see—doesn't reflect our values and yet actually shapes our imagination. And we have to ask ourselves: Who's approving those rape scenes in all the TV shows? Who's filming them? Who's writing those scripts? That's all culture, and culture shapes politics. It's time for us to get our power back. The giants are tumbling, but we have to be able to replace them."

Shift culture through art

"Culture shifts usually happen ten to fifteen years before policy change, which is the last manifestation of an idea that's time has come. And we can't shift culture without artists. Artists are the architects of social change because a politician's imagination is very limited. The artists will help guide us into the future."

Envision abundance

"I love the concept of 'worldview' because we can understand that we all belong. There's enough for all of us, and we have to create systems where we can all thrive. But the ideas have to exist first. We have to imagine and visualize something for behavior to change."

Build power through partnership

"We need a shift toward a regenerative way of being, which is in partnership. That's when we move away from the things that are exploitative to other creatures or to the planet or to people, especially women, around the world. But it's not just women. It's people of color, it's immigrants, it's trans people, it's people with disabilities who are put on the bottom in service to a world of domination. It's very useful for us to think about domination versus partnership because it allows us to imagine building economies that are regenerative and that celebrate partnership, which to me is a very feminist way of looking at the world."

ADVICE TO KEEP GOING

"I feel like when you cultivate a plant it's like a mirror. You give it water and then it grows for you, and then little scales get on it, which you can pick off, and it's kind of metaphoric for picking off all the parasites in your life. And you give it sun. And then, if you don't pay attention to it, like if you don't pay attention to a fern, it starts getting all diva on you. So I think when you learn to care for a plant it's a really good moment for you to connect with another species. It's incredibly grounding and also a way to reduce your stress."

"

I love when people invest energy into something that they can nourish and nurture. It's a good metaphor for your self-care.

"

ISHA CLARKE

BELIEVE IN YOUR POWER

Isha Clarke first stood up against climate injustice in middle school, when a developer wanted to build a coal terminal through a residential neighborhood in their hometown of Oakland, California. Isha recalls going to his office along with other students to protest and intercepting him on his way to the bathroom so he couldn't avoid listening to their demands. In high school, Isha took to an even larger stage by joining members of the Sunrise Movement in US Senator Dianne Feinstein's office to press her to get behind the Green New Deal. The moment was captured in a video that went viral. In 2019, as a high school senior and founding member of the award-winning organization Youth vs. Apocalypse, they helped organize the first-ever youth climate strike in San Francisco. Isha believes we all have the power to reimagine the world and that right now we can, and must, make sure those who hold power see this vision too.

"

Remember, your voice matters and you are important, and this is our future we're talking about. You have every right to stand up and scream for justice.

"

ISHA'S STORY

"As early as I can remember, I listened to my grandpa's stories about his activism. He burned his draft papers and peed in front of the Koch brothers' building, and protested, and has done really incredible things his entire life. Hearing his stories and seeing him lead by example was my earliest introduction to social justice and knowing that I wanted to be like that.

The young people leading [the climate justice] movement have been getting a lot of attention. The fossil fuel industry actually said that we are the number one threat to their way of doing business, which is poisoning the earth, because we've been doing so much: making so much noise, putting so much pressure on them and others like banks and insurance companies that are supporting them in their projects.

Our job [at Youth vs. Apocalypse] is to both redefine what climate justice means and work on the movement from the inside, trying to make sure that frontline voices are always centered. We have a very clear agenda to normalize climate justice and reverse the climate crisis. Historically, communities of color, Indigenous communities, and low-income communities have been targeted. All the oil refineries are put in communities of color. The coal terminals being planned are built through communities of color, and pipelines are built through Indigenous people's water supply and sacred lands.

I realized how central environmental racism is to climate justice and how historically the movement didn't reflect the actual people who were on the front lines of the issue or of the injustice. This is a fight for lives. It's about creating an equitable, just world. And to make sure that the new world that comes forth is sustainable and is run by solutions created by frontline communities."

TOOLS TO CHANGE THE WORLD

Imagine new systems

"Fighting the climate crisis is also fighting all of the systems of oppression that undergird our world and have led us to this crisis. We're taking on the task of completely dismantling everything we know. And that is really scary, and people say it's idealistic. And so I think the largest task is shifting from believing that what we need is idealistic to finding a way to do it."

Resist delay

"We had this action at Chevron and what we were saying was, 'We don't have time for this long, slow transition to renewable energy.' And they were saying, 'You know, well, change is slow.' And, over the course of history, change has been slow. And that's exactly the problem. We need to convince the power holders to change the way that they're approaching things."

Keep the pressure on

"Pressure makes diamonds. Never forget the power we have to put pressure on power holders. Power holders would not have power if it weren't for the people. And so every day as a mantra, as an affirmation, remind yourself that you have power, and that power is multiplied as you link arms with other people and stand in solidarity."

Build momentum

"Find other people who are already doing the work because if you add your energy to a movement that's already happening, it just helps build the momentum. Look for other organizations who are already doing things in your community or close to your community."

ADVICE TO KEEP GOING

Take time for self-reflection by writing out your thoughts

"To be honest, I need to do a better job of giving myself time to do self-care and self-reflect. I'm starting to realize that the only thing that really matters is that you feel comfortable in the body and in the being you are. But that's really hard to do in a society that's telling you what you should do and who you should be all the time. So it takes a lot of self-reflection and self-awareness.

Something I started doing was keeping a journal. I started trying to write every night, and whatever I'm feeling that night is what I'll put in it. So sometimes I'll do a really corny journal entry, and sometimes I'll write a poem, or sometimes I'll make a list. It clears my brain, and that's when I really get to check in with myself and see, 'What was I thinking today?'"

KATE SCHATZ AND MIRIAM KLEIN STAHL

DREAM LIKE A RADICAL

Radical people dream up big, new ideas and protect the hard-won gains that benefit us all. Kate Schatz and Miriam Klein Stahl are the author and artist, respectively, behind a series of *New York Times* best-selling books that feature a number of "rad" women and girls from across the world and throughout history who have fought for change. Miriam and Kate combine powerful stories and hand-cut paper illustrations to bring awareness to those who have succeeded in the face of seemingly impossible odds. From 2015 to 2019, Kate co-led Solidarity Sundays, a national network of feminist activist groups that still meet monthly. In 2022, she coauthored *Do the Work!: An Antiracist Activity Book*, with W. Kamau Bell. Miriam's artwork is as at home on a social movement poster as it is on a museum wall. She is the cofounder of the Arts and Humanities Academy at Berkeley High School in California, where she has taught since 1995, using the arts as a means to understand and address today's challenges and inequities.

KATE AND MIRIAM'S STORY

KATE: "Radicals are people who make waves in their time. They crash against the status quo again and again, eroding resistance until those radical waves ripple through time to become the new mainstream. The thing is, even when an 'outlandish' idea like democracy or free speech or equal rights overcomes resistance to become the norm, there will always be those who seek to go back to the way things were before. Which means the job of a radical isn't just to fight the status quo and make new changes but also to vigilantly protect the radical ideas that have benefited us all, like voting rights and the Violence Against Women Act and reproductive rights.

"

Radical does not have an ideology. It means challenging the system and the status quo.

"

I wasn't raised in a radical feminist household, but I had strong women in my life. In middle school, I got into loudly proclaiming my political beliefs. I also grew up in the 1990s and things like Riot Grrrl and a lot of music—female, powerful, strong punk—were really influential. I'd seen Kathleen Hanna of Bikini Kill and P. J. Harvey loudly and boldly proclaiming their feminism and their identity, so that had a big impact on me."

MIRIAM: "When Kate first brought up this idea of 'radical,' I thought about the things I felt were really radical in my youth. As a young person growing up in the '70s and '80s, I aligned with skateboarding and punk rock, and both of those things were about defying what was mainstream."

KATE: "When I had the idea to do our first book, *Rad American Women A–Z*, I knew I wanted to have a strong visual component. I wanted the images to be really bold and reflect the strength of the women we write about. Our books tell stories about powerful, inspiring women from history and today. I didn't want them to be super cutesy. I wanted them to reflect a kind of strength."

MIRIAM: "Images can do things words can't, and people connect to imagery at an emotional level. I think the way we set up our book, with an image and then a bold quote and then a longer-format story, gives many entry points to different aged kids. A three- or four-year-old can look at the picture and maybe identify letters or maybe read the quote. And then as they grow older, they'll go back and see the image that they loved and read the story."

KATE: "Miriam is incredible. She is a magical wizard. The illustrations are all paper cuts. She does them with a piece of black paper, a pencil, and an X-ACTO knife. They are both intricate and detailed, but incredibly simple and straightforward at the same time. I've seen kids flipping through, looking at the pictures, and they'll see something that catches their eye. Then that will lead them to the text. And that's always an exciting moment."

MIRIAM: "Kate and I were meant to meet each other and create books together. Our books speak to the kid that was like me, who needs pictures and is really drawn into a story through images, and Kate's just the best writer—her words bring you in."

TOOLS TO CHANGE THE WORLD

Let intimidation be your fuel

KATE: "So often women get intimidated by people who they think know more than them or are more experienced than them. If you can, move beyond intimidation and actually let it be a motivation. Let it inspire you to do what you want to do."

Challenge yourself

KATE: "Anybody can be a radical. What it means is to tell the truth, pursue what you believe to be true, and be willing to take risks and fail until you get there. What makes it hard is to maybe be the only one, and maybe sound a little bit crazy, and maybe have people really doubt you. It's not for everybody."

MIRIAM: "Like with skateboarding, watching people completely defy gravity—you shouldn't be able to do that. But people are determined and fall and fall and fall and fall until they do it. I see that kind of thing as a radical act: to have an idea and to do it and fail and do it and fail until you don't fail anymore."

Give no Fs

KATE: "When we're seen as women in positions of power, one of the keys is having no Fs to give. You are just willing to get up there and say your piece and do your thing. And it's what makes people really uncomfortable. But it also makes change happen."

Reflect backward

KATE: "One of the biggest mistakes we can make in our political activism and our drive for social change is to operate in a vacuum, where we don't acknowledge everything that's come before because that's how we learn the lessons. And it can be depressing when someone else was doing exactly this for the same reason and problem a hundred years ago. But it can also be humbling and inspiring to see yourself taking action as part of a continuum and a lineage."

Practice radical kindness

MIRIAM: "I think being kind is a radical act, and it's something I try to practice every day even if I'm having a hard time. To counter the hostility happening around us, just being kind to the people that you're around every day is a really important act of radicalism."

ADVICE TO KEEP GOING

Read history. Make art.

KATE: "I really, really love reading about history. That actually calms me. It gives me a lot of perspective. So the research I've been able to do for our books in times of great national distress has kept me sane. It really gives me a great deal of perspective on how we got here. It's a form of empowerment. I like learning about these really great things that have happened in the face of totally gnarly, ridiculous stuff."

MIRIAM: "For me it's making art. I like to make images. I feel like it's my part. It's the way that I can contribute. It's the thing that comes easy to me, I love doing it, and it brings me joy and peace."

EVE RODSKY

REIMAGINE THE ROLES

The invisible work that married women take on can infiltrate even the most feminist of households. When Eve Rodsky documented every single household chore that took her more than two minutes, her final spreadsheet included over a thousand tasks. She called this list "Shit I Do" and emailed it to her friends and her husband. Her friends shared their resentment at the length of the eye-opening list. Her husband replied with an eye-covering emoji.

She realized this division of labor required a radical shift. So Eve, a Harvard-educated lawyer and mediator, interviewed hundreds of hetero couples, along with economists, psychologists, historians, and neuroscientists to invent a new system. In her best-selling book *Fair Play*, she shows us a world that equally values men's and women's time. Her latest book, *Find Your Unicorn Space,* goes one step further, showing us how to pursue what makes us happiest without guilt or shame. Eve is also the founder of the Fair Play Policy Institute and cofounder of The Careforce, both of which advocate for equitable paid leave and caregiving policies.

EVE'S STORY

"I'm a product of a single mom. At seven years old I was her partner, her parental child. I learned how to use her checkbook to pay her bills. I managed her eviction notices. I vowed that this was not going to happen to me, that I would have a true partner in life. And I did. I married that partner, and we were killing it in business and in life. My husband, Seth, was very supportive of my career. We took turns doing the dishes. We took turns making each other dinner. And then, two kids later, I find myself sobbing on the side of the road over a text he sent me that said, 'I'm surprised you didn't get blueberries.'

I had just had my second son, Ben. My son Zach was three at the time. I had a breast pump in a diaper bag on the passenger seat of my car. I had gifts for a newborn baby to return in the backseat of my car. I had 'opted out'—and I put that in quotes now because I learned that I did not opt out. Society pushed me out of the traditional workforce. I had just started my new firm. I had a client contract in my lap. I had a pen that was stabbing me in the vagina as I was racing to pick up Zach from his toddler transition program, and I'm on top of this chaos where the space-time continuum was sort of collapsing on me.

And so I pull over to the side of the road that day thinking to myself, *I used to be able to manage employee teams, and now I'm so overwhelmed I'm not even managing a grocery list.* More importantly, how did I become the shefault—the default for most of the cognitive labor, the conception and planning for literally every single household and childcare task? That was not supposed to happen to me."

TOOLS TO CHANGE THE WORLD

Recognize all time as equal

"As a society, men, women, and children view men's time as finite, like diamonds. And we view women's time as infinite, like sand. Women are the worst purveyors of these toxic time messages. Unless we retire these old tropes and we start creating an understanding that all time is created equal—then nothing I can say after this, no practical solution, is going to matter."

Visualize a new paradigm

"This is not a partner against partner issue. This is a systemic issue. It is our cultural understanding that we guard men's time. So of course, if my time is guarded, I would want to keep it guarded. I wouldn't even necessarily see the problem. But what is happening now is the invisible work, the mental load, the second shift, the unpaid work is finally visible. That, to me, is the silver lining. But we can't stop there. It does require a system shift."

Show what change looks like

"In Davos, I asked all these male world leaders to—when they got home—tell their child's school to make them the number one person to call when their child is sick. The more we see men modeling and picking up the phone during work meetings to show that their work and life are integrated, the better we'll do. If we just talk about it as women for the next hundred years, nothing will change."

Be a cultural warrior

"It requires empathy for us all to have a cultural shift, to know that an hour holding our child's hand is as valuable as an hour in the boardroom. And that requires us all being cultural warriors. Just by showing up you are a cultural warrior in this movement to recognize the value of care and that all time is created equal. We can't go back if it becomes a movement."

ADVICE TO KEEP GOING

"What is your creative space that makes you uniquely you, and how do you share that with the world? I call it 'unicorn space' because it's like the mythical equine. It's this beautiful, creative space that we used to have before kids and partnerships. But it doesn't exist unless we reclaim it.

It's not sitting there, scrolling for hours on Instagram. It's the active pursuit of what makes you you. It can be crocheting dolls or baking pies. It's about getting that freedom and permission from yourself to be unavailable without guilt or shame. It's about being proud of ourselves and feeling a little bit like we were before we had these roles of parent, partner, and worker.

"

What is your creative space that makes you uniquely you?"

"

I will say that, when I was in 'blueberries time,' right when I was sobbing on the side of the road, anytime someone would forward me a 'find your passion' article, I would say, 'That's just another thing I don't have time to do. So thank you for shaming me. You want me to have self-care? Great. Then you take my kids to school. You try and get some self-care time.' So I only believe in unicorn space in the context of domestic rebalance. Only in that context alone."

LILY TOMLIN

EMBRACE YOUR FEMINIST IDEALS

The entertainment industry thrives on conformity, formulas, and stereotypes. It's rare to find an actress who is rewarded for doing things her own way. But many of Lily Tomlin's early major successes were ones she created for herself. She has starred in movies, on television, on stage, and has dreamed up new characters for her comedy albums since the 1960s. She fired up a generation of working women with Dolly Parton and Jane Fonda in the 1980 film *9 to 5*, in which she played one of three secretaries who take extreme measures against their sexist boss. She also starred with Fonda in the Netflix original series *Grace and Frankie*, about a unique friendship between two women in their seventies. In the movie *Grandma*, she agrees to help her granddaughter find money for an abortion and learn to stand up for herself. In her own life, Lily consistently stands up for women's rights, animal rights, our planet, and authentic self-expression. In 2015, shortly after the US Supreme Court determined that same-sex couples had the right to marry in all states, she and Jane Wagner, her partner and collaborator of forty-four years, decided that they would take the plunge.

> "
> # Boy, it would be a big help if everybody was more feministly inclined.
> "

LILY'S STORY

"We'd [Jane and I] always viewed the concept of marriage fairly cynically. First of all, it was not open to us, and we just didn't want to imitate the heterosexual community. Once the Supreme Court decision was made, I was constantly asked on the red carpet when I was going to get married, and I'd just say, 'Oh, we'll get married sometime. We haven't decided.' This one young fellow who pestered me, he was very sweet about it and funny, but he would say, 'Are you here to get married this year? You think you're going to get married? Are you going to get married? When are you going to get married?' Finally, I said, 'Well, we're thinking about it.' Then every time I'd go on the red carpet, he'd bring it up. We finally just said, 'Maybe we should get married. It'd be fun, it'd be nice. We have the right to get married; it might mean something to other people who want to get married.' We went out to Van Nuys, California, and got our license, and then we had a girlfriend who was a lawyer marry us. It was all very lighthearted and fun."

TOOLS TO CHANGE THE WORLD

Care about the whole species

"Being feminist in many ways is just being humanist and caring about the species. In the old days, we used to say, 'This is about moving the whole species forward, not just half of it.' I totally believe it."

Be feministly inclined

"I don't think I can make anyone a feminist. They might become a feminist or have feminist ideas and not even know it. I'm more concerned about—although I think it totally ties into feminism—the survival of the planet. With all the cruelty among the factions in the world, I always think, 'Boy, it would be a big help if everybody was more feministly inclined.'"

Work with intent

"As an actor, your complete focus is on the role; you're living from the inside out. You're in no way distracted. You're just living. And even if you're standing aside and watching yourself, you're watching it with full intent."

Pick your battles

"I always hearken to Bob Altman saying to me, 'Giggle and give in.' I was talking with him one day about an editor I was working with who was giving me a hard time about edits. He would say, 'Oh, it can't be done.' I'd say, 'Give me the footage. I'll make the edit work.' Sure enough, I could because I know myself so well, I know right where the syllable could be cut. Anyway, Bob would say, 'Just giggle and give in.' Because in some instances, I don't think it's such a bad idea. You might have a much bigger battle ahead."

ADVICE TO KEEP GOING

"I was in my early twenties, and I was typing market research tapes at all hours of the night at the Plaza Hotel. There was an older woman who did it as well, and she said, 'Do you know who Mildred Natwick is?' I said, 'Yes, I do.' She said, 'Well, someday you're going to get Mildred's parts.' Mildred was a wonderful character actress, just wonderful. She was much older than I was. And I thought to myself, *I can't wait until Mildred Natwick takes a dive. I've got to do something for myself.*

“

I've got to do something for myself.

”

I made up characters and would go to The Improv and do them. That was just a natural evolution. And my big break was I got on *Laugh-In*. On hiatus, you don't make a red cent, and all the other show-kids would have to go on *Match Game* or some game show like that. Instead I would go out on the road. I cultivated a whole other audience working live."

ANNA LAPPÉ

ENVISION THE POSSIBILITIES

Anna Lappé grew up in a household where ideas for sustainable, healthy food were not limited to what was for dinner. Two years before she was born, her mother, Frances Moore Lappé, wrote the best-selling book, *Diet for a Small Planet*, which asserted the simple but radical idea that "hunger is not caused by a scarcity of food but a scarcity of democracy." This book revealed the power of everyday acts to create health for ourselves and our planet. Now Anna is a food justice advocate, author, and adviser to those seeking to transform food systems to benefit the environment, health, wellness, and workers. She has been recognized with the James Beard Foundation Leadership Award, and she was named an eco "Who's Who" by *Time* magazine. Anna's professional journey began when she teamed up with her mom on the thirtieth anniversary of *Diet for a Small Planet* to tell the stories of the social movements, city governments, and communities getting to the root causes of hunger. That book became *Hope's Edge: The Next Diet for a Small Planet*.

"

I am constantly reminded how essential persistence is to all the change we need to make in the world.

"

ANNA'S STORY

"I always profoundly respected the work my mother did—and my father as well. He passed away a number of years ago; he was a medical ethicist and toxicologist, and his work was also close to his heart. But while I so respected their work, I never thought I would follow in my mother's footsteps until I was in graduate school in my mid-twenties.

I was at Columbia University, studying economic and political development. I was at a pivot point, trying to figure out what I was doing with the rest of my life. On the other hand, I had a very clear idea of what my mother should do! I believed strongly she should write a book to revisit the lessons she shared in *Diet for a Small Planet* and that told the stories of places around the world where people were actually building a healthy and sustainable food system. I thought through those stories she could give people a sense of possibility.

So, after much prodding, my mother agreed to write the book, but only if I would help her. I started out as a research assistant and eventually became her coauthor. It was an experience that changed my life: We traveled to India, Bangladesh, Poland, Kenya, France, Brazil, and multiple places in the United States—each place another powerful story of a community addressing the root causes of hunger, fighting for ecological food and farming, sometimes up against incredible odds. I was profoundly moved by the work we witnessed and the stories we were told. And by the time the book was published, I knew that *Hope's Edge* had set me on a life's path I had never predicted.

What I loved about the partnership with my mother on the book and our ongoing work together is its intergenerational nature. I feel it's a model of apprenticeship in a way that we've largely lost in today's society. I learned so much from her about what it takes to write and edit a book, about how to connect with strangers in deep conversation for research. I learned more, and more quickly, by having that experience with her than if I had struck out on my own, trying to do it all by myself. I continue to learn so much through the thought partnership we have."

TOOLS TO CHANGE THE WORLD

Bake values into big ideas

"Our food should reflect our basic core values around an environment that's healthy today, tomorrow, and a hundred years from now. That is respectful of animals and animal welfare. That values workers across the food chain. A food system that supports thriving local economies. And that's not going to make us sick but is actually key to long and healthy lives."

Inspire with information

"The food industry employs some of the brightest minds in child psychology and persuasive tactics. We're up against incredible forces. But the data shows that, when you arm young people with information, they are receptive. You don't just tell them what they should eat, but you actually explain the 'why.' You get them excited about it. You get them exposed to good, healthy food; they can be really savvy consumers of information."

Push innovative policies forward

"Sugary drink taxes are a real policy solution to bring revenue into cities for good things like nutrition education. They are the culmination of decades of activism. In every single place that tried to take this on, the soda industry spent millions fighting attempts to just get taxes on the ballot. There were about nineteen cities that tried to pass a tax on sugar-sweetened beverages before Berkeley, California, successfully did. But people didn't give up. Community groups really came together, and it passed by a whopping 76.2 percent."

Know change is possible

"In my work as a writer, advocate, and now working with funders to resource social change, I am constantly reminded how essential persistence is to all the change we need to make in the world. Whether we're taking on the fossil fuel industry to address the climate crisis, or the palm oil industry to protect peatland in Indonesia, or the junk food industry to protect kids' health—we're up against ridiculously deep-pocketed adversaries. And yet, despite the tilted playing field, David does sometimes beat Goliath."

Believe in what you have to say

"The best piece of advice I've gotten about getting out there boldly with my message came from a friend who was a seasoned public speaker. It was just before I gave one of my first public talks, to an audience of 3,000 people! I was terrified, needless to say, and told her as much. She said, 'Anna, you may not ever get over being nervous before you give a public talk, but get in touch with the part of you that knows you have something really important you want people to know. And the rest of it, you can just let it all go.' "

ADVICE TO KEEP GOING

"It was on a research trip for *Hope's Edge* that I had an epiphany about where my own hope and motivation comes from. I'll never forget a conversation with Afsar Jafri, one of the leaders in India who was teaching organic farming in regions that had been sold, for decades, on chemical-intensive industrial agriculture. I asked him, 'Where does your hope come from? Look at what you're up against.' And he looked at me and said, 'For me, doing this work is what gives me hope.' His words have stayed with me all these many years later."

"

Hope does not come from seeking evidence we're winning this big fight because the obstacles are so huge. Hope comes from the work itself. It's inherently energizing.

"

PREPARE

ASSEMBLE YOUR RESOURCES AND
SUMMON YOUR BRAVERY

When you know what you want to change and are ready to move forward, it's time to make a plan and trust in what's possible. Take stock of the skills you have, gather your people, and decide what risks you are willing to take.

The innovative women in this chapter get outside their comfort zone, ask hard questions of themselves and others, and lead with curiosity. They push back on existing systems and beliefs, build on lessons from the past, and lay the groundwork for the future. Their advice to keep going: embrace adventure, work together, build self-esteem, and take the time to refuel.

SEANE CORN

START WITH YOURSELF

When you reflect on your intentions and practice empathy, you can be more present for yourself and more supportive of others. Self-awareness is not just a buzzword. It's a prerequisite for an equitable and just future. Seane Corn, an internationally acclaimed yoga instructor, activist, and author of *Revolution of the Soul*, teaches that without self-awareness our beliefs and actions can unwittingly contribute to the problems we hope to solve. She trains social justice leaders to turn inward to understand their own inherent biases. Whether your focus is climate injustice, poverty, violence against women, racism, or economic inequality, changing the world requires us all to recognize and reject our own harmful practices.

"

The time is now for all of us to wake up and do what needs to be done.

"

SEANE'S STORY

"Yoga itself is a philosophy. One of the main belief systems is that our liberation is bound together: I can't be free unless we're all free. If I believe that, then my actions have to actually manifest that. And I have to be willing to look at the ways in which I'm participating in that separation.

I speak to people like myself, who are white, privileged, able-bodied, with access to resources within the communities of yoga and spirituality. They talk about, 'Let's go out and change the world. Let's be of service.' But to really unpack what that means is complex and messy. For years I wanted to help until I realized that my helping was just one more form of saviorism. My helping without really understanding colonization, without understanding white supremacy, without understanding power dynamics, was just contributing to systems that have already created so many problems.

And yet at the same time, I want to help. I want to do good. I had to dismantle within myself the image I have of myself as a good person to that as a whole person with faults and graces.

We are informed by our history, by our traditions, by our ancestors, by our culture. We hold in our bodies belief systems that live deep within our tissues. So if I'm out in the world and there's conflict and chaos and I get afraid, the rational part of my brain is going to shut down. The reactive part of my brain gets alerted. At that moment, I'm no longer in present time. My nervous system will revert back to the fears of my high school, the fears of my family, the fears of my history. So I have to recognize that's just a reality. I can't not be racist, sexist, homophobic, transphobic. I can't not be ageist or ableist or carry certain biases and discriminatory and stereotypical attitudes because I'm not enlightened, first of all. And because that information is so embodied that, if I'm afraid or tired, odds are that's going to get excavated and cause harm. It might be subtle but is impactful.

If we're really committed to social change, the best gift of allyship that we can give to the world is owning our contribution to its pain and its suffering. That's the first step in."

TOOLS TO CHANGE THE WORLD

Offer service

"Right now in your life, what can you do in order to be of service? Do you have money? Can you support someone who can be on the front line? Can you pay for the lawyers that might be necessary to change the policies that exist? Can you run for local office? There are so many ways in which we can be of service."

Own your mistakes

"Recognize that intention doesn't always equal impact, and we have to take responsibility for the impact we cause that hurts others. Instead of freezing in shame or guilt because we messed up, just acknowledge it, own it, move into it. Commit from your soul to wanting to be a part of this change."

Tap in to your skills

"Get really practical about what your skills are, what your talents are, and what you're being called to do at this time. My experience is that the very place that brought you to your knees, the very place that got you onto the mat or to therapy or into the program where you sought help, support, understanding . . . is the very place in which you will be most skilled to be of service."

Don't let fatigue overwhelm you

"We all have work to do, and we can no longer rely on our national or even global leadership to continue to make choices on our behalf. We have to hold our administration accountable for the choices they are making. We can only do that if we are proactive, if we are engaged, if we are educated, if we're willing to see the bigger picture and not allow ourselves to get overwhelmed or fatigued by the rhetoric continuously coming at us. I believe the fatigue that exists in the world today is politically strategic."

Care for others

"Self-care is critically important, especially for people who are on the front lines, who live on the margins. Their self-care is probably paramount to the work that they're going to do in the world because they're already in such trauma. But that means someone like myself needs to double down so someone else doesn't have to. There are so many things we can do, but apathy is not one of them."

ADVICE TO KEEP GOING

"It's very important to recognize that there's no separation between the mind and the body. Our body remembers everything. It remembers the grief of our grandmothers. It remembers the loss of our mothers. It remembers the heartbreak of every woman who has come before us, and we carry that. It's very much influencing our perspective and the way in which we experience the world and how the world sees us. It's time to honor what our bodies have been holding on to but also be willing to break the cycles for our daughters and for our sons going forward.

"

Build self-esteem, and you will trust your inner guidance.

"

Our work is to reframe our narratives and develop our self-confidence because the thing that blocks our intuition is low self-esteem. Build self-esteem, and you will trust your inner guidance. You might not always like where it takes you, but you will know that's exactly where you're supposed to be, and you will breathe and surrender to it. Knowing that is the gift of being and the challenge of being, and if you can tolerate the discomfort, what's on the other side of it is liberation."

RHEA SUH

CONNECT WITH OTHERS

If you want to tackle big issues, learn the art of collaboration. It isn't always easy to corral multiple points of view and create a dialogue, but it's a critical part of setting up for and sustaining success. Rhea Suh has spent her career building partnerships to protect our climate and the environment. She worked at the Department of the Interior under President Obama and served as president of the National Resources Defense Council during an especially challenging time. Under her leadership, the NRDC was part of a coalition that successfully sued the city of Flint, Michigan, and the state of Michigan for poisoning the water system, to ensure all residents would have access to clean water. When Donald Trump was elected in 2016, she led the push against the incoming administration's intentions to roll back environmental protections. She also facilitated a partnership with the first Women's March to demonstrate that environmental rights and women's rights are inextricably linked.

"

If we don't stand up and fight, if we don't stand together, there's a lot at risk.

"

RHEA'S STORY

"I'm the child of immigrants. My parents came over from South Korea in the immediate aftermath of the Korean War. I think my parents, like lots of other immigrants, were looking for a better opportunity and brighter future for themselves as well as their children, but they were also seeking out a quality of life that they had dreamed about in America.

We found it in Boulder, Colorado. I grew up with the benefit of the natural beauty that is part of our heritage as Americans. I also grew up with a clear recognition that all of those rights, those standards, are not things we can take for granted. As my parents' original home country was demonstrative of, many places around the world don't have those standards or qualities. So we have to defend them, and we have to protect them. That constant process of renewal was built into my DNA from a very early age.

I've since spent my whole career working on environmental policy. And I fundamentally believe that regardless of the fact that this country has become so partisan, and environmental issues have become really partisan, these are ubiquitous values regardless of whether you're a Democrat or Republican in a red state or a blue state.

We care about the air we breathe, the water we drink. We care about this natural heritage that makes America unique. And I think there's an opportunity, in the midst of the crisis that we're facing, to renew that dialogue with Americans.

The Women's March was an opportunity, particularly with the different pillars being represented, for all of us to come together, forge our bonds of resistance and strength, and demonstrate our collective resolve to protect our collective rights. To be with each other, to stand next to each other, to be recognized and noticed, and to set the stage that we're not going to back down. We're not going to step away. We're going to stand up for all the things we believe in."

TOOLS TO CHANGE THE WORLD

Stick to the basics

"A healthy environment is a basic right for all of us. It doesn't matter where we live, what we look like, how much money we make. To translate it down to these basic human rights is something we need to do in much broader and more systematic ways."

Preserve guardrails

"Do we need environmental regulations? Do we need environmental safeguards? Do we need the Environmental Protection Agency? Those things actually matter. They matter to our health. They matter to our quality of life. They matter to the viability of our community."

Know what you're up against

"Make no mistake about the rhetoric around regulatory reform. What that looks like in the real world at the end of the day are situations like Flint. You don't want government regulation? You don't want government enforcement? You don't think these safeguards are important for women, families, children, communities? Then you're going to have many more Flints on your hands. And the reality is I actually think we already have many more Flints on our hands in this country in part due to a failure to maintain infrastructure or to handle a situation that got out of control a long time ago."

> ##
> # Solidarity, companionship, and strength—that's really what it's all about.
> ##

ADVICE TO KEEP GOING

"I think protecting our rights is going to require us to dig deeper and to go places we won't expect. But it's absolutely the fight that's worth having if not for the future of our country, for the future of our children. If we don't stand up and fight, if we don't stand together, there's a lot of risk. So now's the time. Solidarity, companionship, and strength—that's really what it's all about. And let's hope it's the beginning, not the end of how we build these bonds of resistance moving forward."

IJEOMA OLUO

HAVE HARD CONVERSATIONS

If you have privilege, it's easy to relax into existing power structures and perpetuate inequality—even as you intend to fight against it. But it doesn't have to be this way. Author Ijeoma Oluo has won a number of awards for her work confronting deeply uncomfortable truths about racial injustice. She is the *New York Times* best-selling author of *Mediocre: The Dangerous Legacy of White Male America* and *So You Want to Talk About Race.* Her writing shows us that, through clear intentions and a stated agenda, we can embrace difficult conversations, tackle challenges, and begin to shift behavior together—including with those we love the most. That's what happened when Ijeoma finally talked with her mother—who is white—about the role she could play in the fight against racial oppression.

"

A lot of people feel that, because they're feminists, they have some sort of head start in antiracism. But feminists are no more guaranteed to be antiracist than any other white American.

"

IJEOMA'S STORY

"My mom talked a lot about suffering anger and hatred because she was with a Black man. But sitting down to talk about what our respective roles or experiences were from our particular racial viewpoints wasn't the conversation we had. I don't think it's a conversation a lot of families have.

I was shocked and kind of embarrassed to realize I had already spent quite a bit of time encouraging white parents of children of color to talk about race, and my own mom and I hadn't actually really intently driven into that conversation. I think I had assumed my work meant I could skip over it in my personal relationships, that maybe through osmosis other people would just get it. That's not quite how it works.

My mom had a kind of tough early life, and the only place where she really felt accepted and loved was with my father's community, with all of these Nigerians, these Black people. And I think that because my mom had lived so closely with Nigerians for a long time and had loved us and loved our Blackness and loved our heritage so much and had raised us—she really thought that was the same as being Black. She really thought that her place was right next to Black people, next to Blackness, standing with us, dancing with us. Well, she had an invitation to the cookout. But what she didn't get was that she still hadn't lived as a Black person for a single minute of her life, and she didn't quite see what that privilege in her life looked like. She was still just as susceptible to the ways in which privilege stops you from seeing the oppressions of other people.

What she sees herself as now is more as a white person who has a lot of privilege in white spaces to work with other white people to dismantle white privilege. And that's an important shift. It moved her from being someone who was just standing next to me but not really able to do much to help me—other than just be a mom and be a friend, which of course is very important—to being a mom who could find a space in the white world that I don't have access to. To have her own uncomfortable conversations with people and really push for change in spaces that people of color really can't."

TOOLS TO CHANGE THE WORLD

Confront history

"This was a land founded on white supremacy. It is baked into the bones of the society, and that means every institution is built to support and nurture it. As a white person you may not notice, but if you are a person of color it doesn't fit. It rubs against you, and you feel it all the time."

Question power structures

"It's important to realize that we live in a system that's designed to be really easy to fall into power structures. When we look at feminism, the assumption that what white women need is what all women need is baked in from the early days. A lot of people, because of their privilege, haven't stopped to consider, 'Wait a minute, is this really the top concern for all women? And if I say I am working to help all women, then why am I not reaching out to see what every woman needs?' Unless you want to relabel your movement the 'white women movement,' feminism that doesn't practice intersectionality isn't feminism. So if you call yourself a feminist, it's important to remember that that's not an immunization against other bigotries and other biases."

Offer respect over empathy

"Empathy can be limited by how far you can inject your personal experience into something. Even if what they're saying doesn't sound like anything you've experienced, extend respect and say, 'I believe you.'"

Own your share of the work

"Privilege is really obstacles that were moved out of your way and put in front of someone else. As a white person, when you decline to have tough conversations with your neighbors, expect different things from your politicians, or ask hard questions of your boss, you're saying, 'I want to keep it easy for me. And so I will keep it incredibly difficult for other people.' You're just neglecting your share of the work."

"

For me, self-care looks like one day having a world where you could have a break and set some time aside. And we're not there yet.

"

ADVICE TO KEEP GOING

"You know, it's funny. I get this self-care question a lot, but at the end of the day I'm still going to be Black. Either I write about it or I live it. There's no break. I live in a society where racism hits me all the time. That's been my whole life. So I'm not good at self-care—like many people who don't have the luxury of time or a guaranteed escape from these things, I never know when racism is going to hit me.

But I recognize the privilege I have because there are so many other people of color in this country who suffer every day and struggle every day, and also accomplish great things every day and succeed every day. And no one wants to know, and no one wants to hear them. And I at least get to say to the world what is happening in my life and be heard on some level. And that's an amazing privilege that I have. And it's an incredible injustice that not more people of color have that as well."

REBECCA TRAISTER

FOCUS YOUR FURY

Women learn early and often to suppress our strong feelings lest we not be taken seriously, or worse, be labeled "hysterical" (or "nasty," as Hillary Clinton was during her 2016 presidential campaign). But Rebecca Traister, a well-known feminist journalist for media outlets such as the *Washington Post*, *New York Times*, *Salon*, and the *New Republic*, believes it's time to get comfortable with anger. She wrote the book *Good and Mad: The Revolutionary Power of Women's Anger* in "real time" in 2017 during Donald Trump's presidency. The book put women's anger, how our society responds to it, and what that means for gender equality in the middle of the national conversation.

"

That anger making your brain boil? That may be driving you to protest or to run for office, strike, or knock on doors? This has a history. It is politically consequential.

"

REBECCA'S STORY

"There were a bunch of people in the early 2000s who started writing about the news and pop culture from a feminist perspective, and I was among them. We were taking great pains after the bitter backlash toward second-wave feminism, which characterized everybody as angry, screaming, men-hating, sexless, humorless harridans, to prove that's not what this new generation of feminism was. And that meant making sure that nothing sounded too angry.

It was later in my career that there was a day when I was so fucking pissed about things I was reading in the news and my own professional situation, I wrote a column out of pure acidic anger. I didn't take any pains to make it prettier. I was just livid, and I submitted it. Much to my surprise, my editor at the time at the *New Republic* was like, 'This is great!' and published it.

That piece happened to go viral. It was a tremendous lesson to me about the communicative power of anger. It wasn't just something that pushed people away or was divisive. Voicing anger could be meaningful to people who were feeling it but maybe hadn't said it themselves or hadn't heard it from somebody else. It could create connection."

TOOLS TO CHANGE THE WORLD

Calculate the risks

"I am not suggesting other women just go out and rage. If you want to and you feel safe voicing your anger, then I encourage it. But there are very real tolls, risks, and censure. You may be angry because of the way that you're treated at work, but if you go in and express that anger, you risk getting fired or getting a reputation as difficult or crazy in a way that is going to imperil you economically and professionally. If you are a woman of color who is pulled over or questioned about something that is ridiculous, you have every reason in the world to be livid. But if you express that anger, that puts you at risk of not only arrest and incarceration but also injury and death. There are real tolls out there imposed on women who unapologetically express their rage."

Take women's anger seriously

"The anger of men is understood to be pointing you toward something that needs to be fixed, whereas the anger of women suggests that it's the women themselves that need to be fixed. We need to change that. We need to start treating women's anger as an expression that can direct us toward something that's wrong. What does this woman's anger tell us about what's wrong with the world? And how do we take seriously the thing that's making her angry?"

Respond to anger with curiosity

"The only way that we can begin to alter the reception that women's anger gets is to change the way we listen. Be curious about why other women are angry. Understand that for many of us, especially white women and privileged women, some of the anger is going to be directed toward us. We need to think about the validity and political implications of other women's anger. We need to respect it more."

Look to existing leaders

"Women of color have been out on the front lines, never apathetic, never not being angry or working toward organizing and changing this country. But there is a pattern in this country in which relatively privileged white women become angry in moments where it boils over and the injustices become visible and undeniable. They then come into movements and either appropriate or eclipse or assume that they are the leaders. Instead, think about what it means to participate but not be the only one talking. Look to the leadership and work that's already been done by those who have been engaged for a lot longer."

Prepare for pushback

"If we could solve this without tremendous, powerful, destructive, punitive pushback, we would have a long time ago. The whole point is that we're straining against enormous amounts of power held by a minority. This is not something that's going to be fixed in weeks. There are generations of people who have come before us who have given their lives to trying to make this country better. Rather than be depressed by this, I am inspired by the idea that there were people who devoted their lives to this and now it's our turn."

ADVICE TO KEEP GOING

"Within a political and organizing context, anger makes women audible to each other. One of the strategies behind suppressing women's anger is to keep them in isolation and not comparing notes about everything that pisses them off and then perhaps working in cooperation to organize to change those things.

"

It's okay to be angry.

"

It's okay to be angry. It can be correct to be angry. But I also want you to care about other people's anger. It's especially true for me as a white mother of white girls. It's not just, 'I want you to go out and express your anger,' but I want you to care about the anger of the people around you and your friends and compatriots. I want you to express your anger to each other and learn to value it and work together."

CAROLINE PAUL

TRAIN TO BE BRAVE

Have you ever thought about climbing the Golden Gate Bridge, untethered, for fun? Or getting into *Guinness World Records* for crawling? Or training for the Olympic luge team? Caroline Paul has done every one of these things and more. She wants each of us to try things that might scare us, change how we think about risk, and cultivate our gutsiness. In 1989, Caroline was one of the first female firefighters in San Francisco, California—1 of 15 women out of a crew of 1,500. For over thirteen years, every working day was an adventure. After retiring, she published a memoir about her experience and now makes her living as a writer. Her books include *You Are Mighty*, which provides tools for young activists to stand up and make change, and *The Gutsy Girl*, in which she not only documents her adventures but also shares what she's learned to inspire more adventures for everyone.

"

I'm not against fear.
I'm just pro-gutsy.

"

CAROLINE'S STORY

"I was a kid that was really shy, but I had a twin sister who was very outgoing and very social, so she was my buffer for a long time. I also read a lot of books about adventure. And adventure taught me a lot about how to manage fear.

I grew up in a really hands-off era for kids. It wasn't until recently that I realized I should be crediting my mother for my adventurous lifestyle because she told me very recently that she had grown up with a very fearful mother. Then, at twenty-one, she went on a ski trip with friends, and it was a revelation. She had so much fun and realized everything she'd been missing because her mom had kept her and her sister from doing things like that. She didn't want the same for us. So she encouraged us to do everything; she wanted us to find what we wanted to do.

I never thought I would be a firefighter when I was growing up. When I was in my twenties, I thought I was going to be a documentary filmmaker or a radio person. I was a volunteer at KPFA [a radio station in Berkeley, California], doing the morning news. At the time all these stories were coming over my desk about the racism and sexism in the San Francisco

Fire Department. So I thought, *Maybe I'll go get an undercover story, and I'll pretend I'm interested in being a firefighter and take the test.* To my surprise, I got in. And by then I was really quite intrigued with the fire department; it seemed like it would fit my personality. It was an adventurous life. So I became a firefighter, and I loved it.

It was a homogenous institution that was a thoroughly male culture. Initially my attitude was, I don't have to prove myself. And then one of the women who had come in in the first class set me straight. She said, 'Caroline, guess what? You have to prove yourself every day.' And she was right. And it wasn't that the men were bad. It was just that it was an institution that didn't believe women could do the job.

When you came in, you had to adapt to a very male definition of bravery and courage. And if you didn't, you were often judged to be weak. So a woman who gives her ax to somebody ahead of her because he has a better place to work is going to be viewed as someone who doesn't want to work. The ritual was to push your way to the front of the line. You say, 'I can do it.' That's very against what most of us women have been brought up to do. So it took a long time to learn that kind of thing."

TOOLS TO CHANGE THE WORLD

Notice your own gender biases

"If you have a daughter and a son, notice how you're raising them differently when it comes to challenges, especially physical challenges. And then once you notice, ask yourself, are you really protecting her when you caution her and instill this idea of fear? I think the best way to protect them is to give guidance on how to deal with danger and deal with situations outside their comfort zone."

Embrace exhilaration

"The thing about fear is that it actually feels a lot like excitement physiologically. You might be jittery and flushed, and your heart's racing and you think that's fear. In fact, it's exhilaration, and you're deciding not to do something and missing out on a lot of fun. I really want girls and women to start training on bravery because it is something that's learned."

Believe you can

"As women, we're taught to come from this paradigm of fear and caution, and to make this long list of everything that can go wrong and really give it credence. Girls and women are always underestimating their abilities. Men, on the other hand, overestimate their abilities. There must be a way where you can actually estimate your abilities correctly, so you take more risk."

Go for gutsy

"You have to come from a place of bravery where you're actually looking at your skills, looking at the situation, looking at all your emotions, and looking at your fear. Fear is good. It keeps you safe. I'm not against fear. I'm just pro-gutsy."

ADVICE TO KEEP GOING

Take time for fun

"I used to go all around the world, having adventures. I've been to Siberia, Borneo, and Australia. And then a friend of mine said, 'You know, Caroline, the best wilderness is in the United States.' And he was right on that. You can have adventures really close to home. I think that an adventure is when you get outside your comfort zone and you're also having fun."

TIFFANY SHLAIN

SLOW DOWN AND UNPLUG

Sometimes the best way to achieve a breakthrough is to simply take a break. Tiffany Shlain is an Emmy-nominated filmmaker, author, and founder of The Webby Awards whose work covers gender equity, reproductive rights, and the science of creativity. Her films have appeared on screens large and small. Yet this internet pioneer has nourished her own creativity and activism for more than a decade by taking time for what she has named a "Tech Shabbat"—turning off all screens from Friday night to Saturday night. This life-changing approach led her to write the best-selling book, *24/6: Giving up Screens One Day a Week to Get More Time, Creativity, and Connection*, which shows us how we can all reclaim perspective, be more present with our family, and have more energy to make the change we want to see in the world.

"

If you're running a million miles an hour, you're never going to recharge and you're not going to be as effective.

"

TIFFANY'S STORY

"I had this really intense time when my father was diagnosed with brain cancer and I learned I was pregnant in the same week. In those nine months I thought a lot about life and death and what we're doing when we're here. Whenever I visited my dad, who was quite sick, I would turn off my phone. And then he passed away, and my daughter was born days later, and my husband and I just knew we wanted to change the way we were living. Shortly after that we participated in a National Day of Unplugging, which is one ceremonial day a year of turning off the screens. We had this really wonderful night, and the next day just felt so good. It was the cleanest day. It was the longest day. It was the most present and happiest I'd been in a long time. And we never stopped doing it.

With our Tech Shabbat the benefits just multiply and amplify. I feel very creative, and I laugh a lot more. I just feel like I'm there for the funny. I feel more connected to myself, to my kids, my husband. It's this day every week that is so important to us and grounds us.

And on Saturday night I re-appreciate the marvels of this miraculous tool called the web and technology all over again.

Shabbat is a very old practice from our people. We're Jewish, but we are cultural Jews, not religious Jews. So we are abiding by our own modern twist, which is no screens. But it was such a radical idea. A day of rest—it's the fourth commandment, above 'Do not commit murder.' After six days you shall rest for a whole day. It's such deep wisdom and it's thousands of years old. It's free. It's available to everyone. I would love for people to engage with a full day of Shabbat."

TOOLS TO CHANGE THE WORLD

Put your mind in a different mode

"[Tech Shabbat] is literally something I run toward now. I can't wait for it. And I feel like I remember how to live in a different way. They say for creativity it's good to put your mind in a different mode, even if it's just one day a week. And every week it just feels like this very deep relaxation and different mood that carries me over to the next week."

Pull away from the noise

"By taking a day for yourself, you're going to be that much more able to do your activism. These are all marathons. And if we're running a million miles an hour, 24/7 activism, you're never going to recharge and you're not going to be as effective."

Find perspective

"You have to find the joy in life to keep going. I find most of my joy on Saturdays. I am usually out in nature. I'm seeing that I get the perspective that I don't feel like I have the other six days."

Be present

"Remember how incredible it is to be really present for the people around you instead of the people or the things happening on the phone."

ADVICE TO KEEP GOING

"It's great to be reachable. It's just not great twenty-four hours, seven days a week. It's good to have a day where you're not going to be reachable to every news headline, every family member, every text alert. I love being available the other days, but I need a day to just ground myself. To me, the power is that we do this every week.

"

I think people forget how good it feels to not be so reachable.

"

It's the best thing I've ever done in my life. Just try this very simple practice, and I promise you it's going to make you feel better about the way you're living."

CREATE

PUT IT ALL TOGETHER

Trust in your power to make your dream of change a reality. Your experiences give you the perspective to bring your plan to life in a unique way. Stay focused with purpose, persistence, and courage.

The trailblazing women in these stories will inspire you and motivate you. They are undaunted by what others think, driven by a passion for their work and a commitment to their goals. They sustain themselves through laughter, rest, and self-acceptance.

MARGARITA QUIHUIS

CREATE WITH THE FUTURE IN MIND

It's one thing to dream of world peace and entirely another to create the tools to engineer it. Margarita Quihuis is leading a new field called peace tech in which she does just that. She is familiar with being at the forefront of change. Native American (Yaqui) on her father's side, she was the first person in her working-class Mexican American family to go to college. She was also the first person from her high school to attend Stanford. Now she leads Stanford's Peace Innovation Lab and Peace Innovation Institute at The Hague. She and her team work with businesses, entrepreneurs, governments, and educators to incorporate technology into products and practices that promote and measure peace. This includes everything from designing video game player interactions to be more civilized, to preventing hate crime, to incentivizing welcoming environments for immigrants and refugees. She also leads PeaceX Ventures, which invests in companies built from the ground up to be sustainable, diverse, and ethical. In everything she does, Margarita is creating tools to tackle audacious goals and improve our everyday interactions.

"

When we can measure whether or not something works, we can start moving the needle in the direction that we want.

"

MARGARITA'S STORY

"I'm working on world peace.

I'm using behavior design and innovation methods to figure out how people can learn to work together at scale to solve problems, measurably reduce human violence, and increase positive engagement across conflict boundaries.

In peace studies, there are two types of peace. There's negative peace and there's positive peace. When most people think about peace studies, they think about conflict. And so we have hundreds of years of interventions around that. We have trade sanctions. We build up our defense departments, we use intimidation, we bomb people. We do all those things. That's all negative peace. It's basically someone's done something bad. And so we're going to do something bad back to them so they'll stop doing the bad thing. How am I going to keep the peace? I'm going to bomb the hell out of you, right? That's negative peace.

Positive peace is something generative, where the question is, how good can we be to each other? So if you think about health, you have disease and you have wellness. Diseases are like negative health. I'm going in and I'm doing an intervention to fix something that's broken. Wellness is about saying, 'How much healthier can you be?' And so the negative peace and the positive peace are that mirror image. We're focusing on how we get people to communicate, cooperate, collaborate, and innovate. If we can get people to do this, we can have more peace in the world."

TOOLS TO CHANGE THE WORLD

Integrate different perspectives

"I'm going to be attuned to something in the environment that you're not because of my upbringing, my cultural sensitivity. Everyone has a different focus and will bring to the surface something that you should know—but if you're not tuned in to it, you're completely oblivious. It's really important for the collective survival of humanity that we be able to listen to each other. To be aware and say, 'What do you see that I'm not seeing?'"

Generate happiness

"At the end of the day, everyone wants to have a happier life. And if we can help people do that, the need for conflict goes away. Because I don't have a grievance anymore. I'm innovating, I'm being creative, and I'm being generative with people who are different from me because that way we can have some sort of exchange."

Cultivate positive purpose

"In countries where there's a lot of conflict, the majority of the population is under thirty. They're very young and can't see a future for themselves. And so they're vulnerable to narratives that say, 'I'm going to give you a cause to join that is bigger than yourself.' That works for the dark side, and it works for the light side. The problem is we haven't invested enough on the light side to give people an alternative. So that's what we're working toward."

Look for long-term solutions

"For an issue like refugee integration or immigrant integration, if societies don't do that well, they're just creating trouble for themselves fifteen and twenty years down the road. It's actually in your best interest to embrace them, figure out how to onboard them, how to make them feel welcome so they can feel like productive members of society."

"

If you can imagine the future, why not imagine an amazing future?

"

ADVICE TO KEEP GOING

"When we look at society, how do we get people to feel like they have agency? That they have a narrative and hope in their life, something that they can aspire to? If you can imagine the future, why not imagine an amazing future? Once you start putting that image in your head, then all your behaviors start aligning to do that. It's sort of a Jedi mind trick you can do on yourself."

ILYSE HOGUE

LEAD WITH COURAGE

Ilyse Hogue is an expert mobilizer of social justice movements and progressive causes. From 2013 to 2021, she led NARAL Pro-Choice America, where she focused on mainstreaming abortion rights and reproductive freedom in the face of continuous legal threats and personal harassment. She has also worked to ensure people have access to contraception, family planning, parental leave, and the right to make decisions about their bodies, free of stigma and shame. In her 2020 book, *The Lie That Binds*, she looks at the erosion of reproductive freedom by the radical right as a precursor to the erosion of democracy. Even though the majority of Americans support legal access to abortion, the conservative majority of the US Supreme Court overturned Roe v. Wade in 2022, sparking outrage, spurring protest, and limiting human rights.

When presidential candidate Donald Trump said in 2016 that women who had abortions should be punished, Ilyse posted a picture of herself on Twitter holding a sign that read, "I had an abortion #wontbepunished" and encouraged others to do the same. This brave act sparked thousands more to join her rallying cry.

ILYSE'S STORY

"What allows the antichoice minority to thrive is the sense that we should have shame around talking about our own abortion stories. Abortion is a real piece of life for so many women in this country. And yet people are silent because of the shame. So I wanted to use that moment and illustrate that I was one of them. And, you know, I always say it's a chapter in my life. It's not the novel of my story. I wanted Donald Trump and everyone else running for office, and every woman who has felt shame about her own personal choices because of what society heaps on us, to actually see that we have nothing to be ashamed of.

[When I took the position at NARAL,] I never saw myself as an advocate specifically for women's rights, much less reproductive rights. I had been evolving my consciousness through all of the social justice work I had done, both internationally and here at home, around what it means to have women in leadership roles and for women to be able to fully participate in civil society.

What I have come to understand is that there is no way to have an authentic conversation about women's full participation unless it starts with the idea that we have autonomous decision-making power about how, if, and with whom we choose to grow our families. Because when we are forced into situations that are not of our own choosing, the reality is that everything else we aspire to fades from view.

When women are offered access to participate equally in society and business and the government, not only do they individually thrive but their families thrive and our country thrives. All the data bears this out. So there's a human rights element to it that's actually a proxy for equality and empowerment."

TOOLS TO CHANGE THE WORLD

Force accountability

"Policy makers need to know that there are people who are going to support them when they're out there doing the right thing. And our opponents need to feel political consequences. That comes through people power: people being engaged and doing the day-to-day work of holding their policy makers accountable."

Drive the agenda

"If we can organize women, what will open up is a huge opportunity to discuss what a reproductive freedom agenda looks like in the 21st century. What it looks like to have real policies that support women living real lives right now. And that can make everything better for everyone."

Know your opposition

"Since the day that *Roe v. Wade* gave women the constitutional right to make their own decisions about carrying a pregnancy to term or not, there has been an organized opposition seeking to roll that back by any means possible. And one of the things that they have realized is that when they state their truth and say that their agenda is to outlaw abortion, they lose because we live in a country where the majority of people—whether or not they personally identify as thinking they would have an abortion, whether they are male or female, whether they identify as Republican or Democrat—believe in legal access to abortion and that this is a decision best left to women."

Find common ground

"People may have a lot of mixed feelings about what it means to make the decision to terminate a pregnancy, but still stand strong that this is an individual decision and that a politician who knows nothing about your life should not be making it for you. There's a lot of common ground there because we recognize our own humanity, the humanity of others, and how life is complicated. And when life gets complicated, we want to support others making difficult decisions."

"

Always come from a place of optimism and opportunity. That is what keeps me inspired to do the work that I do and also motivates people to want to work alongside you.

"

ADVICE TO KEEP GOING

"The crisis can actually awaken people, but the opportunity is what keeps people engaged in the long haul. And that's what I'm excited about. The other advice I got about standing up for my beliefs is to keep my eyes on the horizon. You know, we're fighting for not just what we've won in the past but a better future. The more that we are actively engaged in defining that future, the more we offer opportunities for people to get engaged and join that fight."

THE KITCHEN SISTERS (DAVIA NELSON AND NIKKI SILVA)

COLLABORATE. IT'S FANTASTIC.

Finding a partner to work with can lead to extraordinary ideas and the encouragement to experiment. Davia Nelson and Nikki Silva (together known as The Kitchen Sisters) are Peabody Award–winning radio producers, recognized for their public radio series *Hidden Kitchens, The Hidden World of Girls*, and other audio documentaries that feature under-represented voices, cultures, and traditions. Their collaboration began just after graduating from UC Santa Cruz. It was the 1970s, in the midst of the antiwar movement. Nikki was working in the local museum, curating exhibits and record-ing the stories of older people in town. Davia was one of only a few women with a show on the local radio station. Intro-duced by a mutual friend, they first met up on the museum porch, where they talked for hours, "just kind of falling in love," as Nikki describes it. They decided to produce oral histories together, and pioneered an approach that is now a model used by audio producers around the world.

"

We both do great things separately, but we do something else together, which is bigger than either of our visions.

"

DAVIA AND NIKKI'S STORY

DAVIA: "Nikki and a group of people had bought land together and a house—starting what has become a commune that is still in existence some thirty years later. One day, she went down the hill to the KOA campground to get some milk. And there was the Road Ranger. He was dressed in a gray, one-piece jumpsuit, had this huge belt, this ten-gallon hat in his Ford Ranchero pickup truck on this windy stretch of road between San Jose and Santa Cruz on Highway 17. He was a Vietnam vet named Alan Little, and he came back from the Vietnam War and just wasn't done fighting. He needed to still be in a uniform, and he found this persona, the Road Ranger, champion of the stranded traveler.

Nikki took one look and arranged the interview. We went on patrol with him, and that's what led us in to this whole thing."

NIKKI: "We didn't really do it thinking we were going to put it on NPR. Actually, we didn't know anything about NPR. It wasn't in our town. We'd barely heard it. I think that might've been the first time too, when we put some music underneath the voice and we thought, 'Oh my gosh, yeah, let's do this.'

We reconstructed him saving a stranded traveler at the top of the mountain on Highway 17. And we made every mistake in the book. We recorded him in a Denny's where we met him to go on patrol. There's all this clanging of dirty dishes and ambient music in the background.

We had this really long microphone cord, and he kept running over it. And Davia had white pants on, and at one point when he was blowing through his air filter or whatever, this oil spread out all over her pants. So we always say, 'Never wear white pants on patrol.'"

DAVIA: "Rules to live by."

NIKKI: "Sacrificing for the cause. I mean, we made every mistake you could make, trying to do a really good radio documentary on that first story."

TOOLS TO CHANGE THE WORLD

Seek out unheard perspectives

DAVIA: "Nikki and I share a love of the quest and love of bringing voices out that people in the media don't always seek out, whose perspectives and voices wouldn't be heard. We're both possessed by that."

Experiment for fun

NIKKI: "We started to teach ourselves to cut tape, and there weren't many people doing that at our station. So we were experimenting and fooling around and trying to figure it out for ourselves. We would play these little bits and pieces on our weekly show. We'd interject live interviews and music, and then play something we'd recorded; we'd interview a filmmaker or whoever was passing through town."

Listen to learn

NIKKI: "We asked questions, but as we progressed, we began cutting our voices out and we found that allowed the listener to be there rather than us being in between the listener and the teller. We always kind of thought that we were making little movies with our radio shows. It was great to move out of the frame and let the main person be the teller."

Push back on pushback

NIKKI: "One of the few pieces we sent in to NPR they wouldn't air; it was the story of the world champion, one-armed pool player, Ernie Morgan, who came through our town. He was doing this great show at one of the seedy bars in town. We wanted to document it, and we didn't put our voices in. We took our voices out. And they told us, 'Well, you can't do this. You know, you have to lead with, "We're in a smoky barroom," you know, and dah, dah, dah, dah.' We said, 'Well, how did you know we were in a smoky barroom?' And it ultimately did get aired."

ADVICE TO KEEP GOING

Stick together and trust each other

NIKKI: "This level of commitment is like a marriage; it's like any relationship. It's got its highs, and it's got its lows, and it's hard. There are very distinct things that happen in a collaboration. I think it's commitment, love, and belief. It's nice to be doing it with someone else—a friend and somebody you love and trust."

DAVIA: "We just get caught in the love and the passion for the stories, and what we feel has to be done and told."

HEATHER McTEER TONEY

ENGAGE THE NEXT GENERATION

The actions we take today will have an impact for generations to come—especially when it comes to environmental policies and practices. When Heather McTeer Toney was just twenty-seven, she was elected as the first African American, first female, and youngest mayor of her hometown, Greenville, Mississippi. She served two terms, from 2004 to 2012, and focused on sustainable infrastructure. She then worked in the Obama administration as the regional administrator for the Environmental Protection Agency in the Southeast. It was there she learned about Moms Clean Air Force, an environmental advocacy organization. She worked with them to create a program linking mayors with moms who wanted to become more active in their local communities. As a mother with a new baby herself at the time, this role brought her experience in politics and environmental justice full circle. She went on to lead community engagement for the Environmental Defense Fund, collaborating with labor, academia, faith-based organizations, and mayors. Her work reflects the values she grew up with, which she in turn is passing along to her own kids.

"

Come on. Wake up.
Let's go, let's go, let's go!

"

HEATHER'S STORY

"I was the little kid you see at the campaigns, running around messing up all the papers. I was that kid at the meetings at seven, eight o'clock at night in the back making noise, playing with the water cups.

My parents are social justice activists. My father is a retired civil rights attorney. My mother is a retired teacher who owned her own business. Between the two of them, this idea of social justice as a way of life is how I was raised. They always made sure both my brother and I understood we were a part of a larger community. There wasn't any elevation of 'you're better than' or 'you're lower than.' To be a true servant, you serve with people and you serve people.

When my dad was out and participating in a march, my brother and I were there too. I have seen pictures of myself in my Sunday best on the front lines, and I'm positive that I was enjoying playing or being around other friends, but I was participating in social justice. That's what it was like in our house.

And that's what it looks like in my house now, which I love. My kids are part of events that we do with Moms Clean Air Force. When my thirteen-year-old, who tends to be the shy type, did her first television interview with a local news station, and I was rushing as the mom to get pictures, I saw exactly what was happening to her, which was the same thing that happened to me. You're around it so much that it comes out of you in ways sometimes that you can't expect. It was one of those teary moments like, 'Oh my God, this is my baby.' And at the same time being extremely proud, I understood how my parents felt about me."

TOOLS TO CHANGE THE WORLD

Show what's at stake

"[Moms Clean Air Force] has an annual 'play-in' for climate action in Washington, DC. Instead of a sit-in we bring our kids, and they are on the Capitol lawn playing, having activities. We're talking about climate justice. We're talking about air pollution. We're talking about the things we need to protect our children. And then we all go to Capitol Hill and visit our members of Congress. We tell them our concerns and demand action and are very specific about our requests. Members of Congress want to stop and take selfies with our kids and with us. And then they promise us they'll do something on this climate action because they know we're serious."

Focus on what's possible

"Stop being in this space of despair. We have a clock, we know the countdown, and we know we also have some really great opportunities. So I cannot in my good conscience let you sit and wallow in despair when I know we have this great opportunity to do positive things. Come on. Wake up. Let's go, let's go, let's go!"

Change hearts

"Even members of Congress who aren't as enthused about the type of climate actions we want respect Moms Clean Air Force because we say that we are 'mom-partisan.' It doesn't make a difference if you're Republican or Democrat, Tea Party, liberal, conservative. That doesn't matter. We want to know all of our members of Congress are doing things that are helpful and healthy to our children."

Champion future changemakers

"Have real conversations about real issues. In today's society, young people are seeing very similar types of issues. That's inclusive of climate. It's inclusive of immigration. It's inclusive of gun violence. We have to have conversations with them because they want to do something. They want to be active. They're seeking our guidance on how to do it, and then they're making their own decisions."

"

How can we talk about giving the earth a break when we won't ourselves sit down?

"

ADVICE TO KEEP GOING

"As women, we have this way of thinking that we have to go 24/7 and use up all the minutes in the day and to do all of the things seven days a week. We are sacrificing ourselves on the altar of getting things done as opposed to ensuring we have some self-care. The more we have those periods of rest—the more we understand we're in this together, that there's a team of people—the more we can get done. It is truly operating as a village, so you can go and take a nap this Saturday because I'm going to pick up your kids and we're going to go to the march because the kids want to go to the march. And then next Saturday they're at your house.

Resting is what rejuvenates us to be able to do the work. It's also reflective of what has to be done. We want our earth to rest. We need to work on not taking so many resources out of the earth and give it a break. How can we walk around and talk about giving the earth a break when we won't ourselves sit down? Self-care is so important, but it's also about sisterhood. It's about family, it's about community. And it's about showing the face of environmental work. And that includes a moment to rest."

SARAH SILVERMAN

DON'T HOLD BACK

When you know where you want to go, it may not be necessary to take the conventional path to get there. But it sure does help to have someone cheering you on. Sarah Silverman is a two-time Emmy Award–winning comedian, actress, writer, and producer. In her first year of college, Sarah was encouraged by her father to opt out so she could focus on her comedy craft instead. Her career took off when she became a writer and performer on *Saturday Night Live* in 1993, when it was still rare to be a woman in the writers' room, let alone to create comedy about the female experience.

She is known for her straight-shooting stand-up comedy as well as for her outspoken activism, which she also delivers with insightful and incisive humor. Her best-selling memoir, *The Bedwetter*, came out in 2010 and was adapted as an off-Broadway musical of the same name by Atlantic Theater Company, which premiered in May 2022. She has been in numerous TV shows and films, including *The Sarah Silverman Program* and Emmy-nominated *I Love You, America with Sarah Silverman*. She explored her dark side in the dramatic film *I Smile Back*, which garnered her a nomination for a Screen Actors Guild Award. On the critically acclaimed *The Sarah Silverman Podcast* she never hesitates to share her unvarnished perspective on everything from abortion to antisemitism to voter suppression.

"

Women who are unafraid to be powerful also aren't afraid to be vulnerable.

"

SARAH'S STORY

"I had been doing stand-up since I was seventeen, and then I finished high school and moved to New York. I passed out flyers for a comedy club for two years, and they let me have stage time. By the time I was nineteen, I was doing stand-up professionally, meaning I got $10 for each spot.

I knew I wanted to be a comedian and an actor, and I was a drama major at NYU, which is an amazing program, but it's a lot of money for something that you don't need a degree to get hired for. And so my dad made a deal with me that if I dropped out of college, he would pay my rent for the next three years as if it were my sophomore, junior, and senior year, and I would continue doing stand-up. It was a good deal because we both realized what I wanted to do didn't take a degree.

I stole classes from NYU after that. They don't know if you're in their class because they're big, giant lecture classes. I took a whole philosophy course; I just didn't pass in any papers. I love learning. I loved taking classes, and I was able to get a lot out of just stealing them, to be honest. By the time I would've graduated, I was hired as a writer on *Saturday Night Live*."

TOOLS TO CHANGE THE WORLD

Explore different sides of yourself

"There are a lot of sides of me, like all of us, and I've always mined darker topics for things I like to talk about in comedy. I think comedians share a darker side, and that's why comedians will do dramas and do a good job."

Speak authentically

"Women have been taking over comedy ever since Tina Fey became head writer at *Saturday Night Live*. She and Amy Poehler and Chelsea Handler and all these really powerful women who are unafraid to be powerful also aren't afraid to be vulnerable. What's important to realize is that I can talk about a female experience. To me, the best comedy isn't second-guessing your audience."

Don't worry about what others think

"I'm trying in therapy to live a life undaunted by thoughts of legacy or mortality, or immortality, or how I'm perceived, or having how I feel about myself be dependent on how people may perceive me. That's a prison. I'm not perfect at it, obviously, but that's what I'm aiming for."

Embrace the quiet moments

"I've gotten a lot of great advice. Garry Shandling gave me great advice about acting and the moments between the lines and not being afraid of the quiet moments."

ADVICE TO KEEP GOING

"I've never been naked in anything until I turned forty, and that worked out well for me because I've grown emotionally. I'm not perfect and I nitpick things about myself, but I mostly know this is my human shell and it's just fine. It's good to show your body. There's nothing wrong with it. It's strong and it works. I mean, I have stood in front of the mirror and lifted my boobs and been like, 'They used to be there. Now they're here.' If you don't at least journey to reconcile with the process of aging and mortality, then life, especially for a woman, is like a very slow-moving horror film."

GLORIA STEINEM

START A REVOLUTION

Take risks, get outrageous, and embrace rebellion—three critical actions to manifest change championed by iconic writer, lecturer, political activist, and feminist organizer Gloria Steinem. A trip to India just after she graduated from college influenced her interest in nonviolent conflict resolution and what she calls "universal guidelines" for community organizing. Gloria has been a leader of the women's movement and the fight for equality since the 1960s. In 2013, President Barack Obama awarded her the Presidential Medal of Freedom. Through her speeches, books, documentary films, and the organizations she's founded, Gloria advocates for reproductive choice and ending violence against women and children. She cofounded the Ms. Foundation for Women, the Women's Media Center, and the National Women's Political Caucus, among others. She also cofounded *New York* magazine and *Ms.*, the first feminist magazine with national distribution, which is still going strong after more than fifty years.

"

Promise yourself that, in the next twenty-four hours, you're going to do one outrageous thing in the cause of social justice and change.

"

GLORIA'S STORY

"National magazines, even today, are not owned, controlled, or edited by women, so when we started *Ms.* in 1972 it was absolutely a very strange idea. The women's magazines were, and still are to a large extent, about fashion and beauty and cooking and pleasing. The thought that we were going to start what we thought of as 'a way of making revolution, not hamburgers,' as Flo Kennedy always said, was very, very, very ridiculed.

Fortunately, we got *New York* magazine, which I had also helped start, to insert a sample issue, which then made it possible to do a preview issue. We were so afraid we were going to disgrace the entire women's movement, so even though it came out in January, we put on the cover that it was a spring edition. We thought it might just lie there like rocks on the newsstands.

Since we didn't have money for publicity, all of the authors spread out across the country on a PR tour. I was in San Francisco doing a morning talk show, and someone called after the show and said it wasn't at the newsstands. And so I called home and said, 'It never got here; it didn't get distributed.'

It turns out it had sold out in eight days."

TOOLS TO CHANGE THE WORLD

Push back against patriarchy

"The majority consciousness has changed to believe that the principle of equality is desirable. That means that there is also a backlash because we're now considered a serious threat to those folks who have been making unfair profits from unequal pay, as well as those who firmly believe that reproduction, women's bodies, and the basic decisions of life should be in male hands, not in female hands. So we both have succeeded and are now on the knife's edge of whether it will continue or not in the way that it should."

Organize in community

"If you want people to listen to you, you have to listen to them. If you want to know how people live, you have to go where they live. Everybody needs to tell their stories, sitting in a circle, being listened to in order to have a community of support and change. It took me a while after I came home [from India] and saw the civil rights movement, the antiwar movement, and then the women's movement to understand that these were universal guidelines."

Balance power

"If you are in a group and you have more power than the other folks in the group, just remember to listen as much as you talk. And if you have less power, remember to talk as much as you listen, which can be just as hard because you're used to hiding."

Learn from Indigenous cultures

"For most of human history and certainly in North and South America, the earliest cultures are matrilineal. Women controlled their own fertility by herbs and abortifacients. Women tended also to control agriculture while men hunted, but those two things were considered equally necessary. In many of the Native American cultures, female elders decided if it was necessary to go to war or when to make peace. They chose the male leaders. They were part of a circular, consultative, consensus-seeking government that was profoundly democratic."

Battle for your body

"It is the basic battle. Controlling our own physical selves, especially for women—for men too—is the first step in any democracy. Either we decide what happens to our bodies, we can use our own voices, or there is no democracy after that."

ADVICE TO KEEP GOING

Laugh as much as possible

"I've figured out in the last few years, although all the old cultures knew this anyway, that laughter is the only free emotion. You can compel fear, obviously. You can also compel love. If you are dependent for long enough, you enmesh with your captor in order to survive. But laughter happens when you learn something, when you think of something. And old cultures—especially Native American cultures—have a spirit of laughter who was neither male nor female, who symbolizes breaking into the unknown. They say laughter breaks into the unknown—that if you can't laugh, you can't pray. So I would just submit that if you use the degree of laughter as proof of freedom, it's a kind of daily guide."

TRANSFORM

CATALYZE CHANGE

When you challenge assumptions, push limits, and flip power structures, what once may have felt impossible becomes transformational.

The groundbreaking women in this chapter take striking actions and voice revolutionary ideas that result in substantive change. They know their "why," solve problems, and challenge systems. To keep going, they advocate for themselves and each other, learn from their losses, and make things better for those who come next.

TERESA YOUNGER

POWER GRASSROOTS MOVEMENTS

Transformational change can come from raising your voice. And it can come from stepping back to listen. When Teresa Younger was in elementary school, she remembers calling out her school bus driver for telling her and other kids of color to sit in the back. As an adult, she has spent her career both speaking up for and building power with those not typically heard. She served as executive director of Connecticut's Permanent Commission on the Status of Women and was the first African American and the first woman to lead the ACLU of Connecticut. Teresa is a lifetime Girl Scout and Gold Award recipient, and was recently inducted into the Connecticut Women's Hall of Fame. In 2015, she became president and CEO of the Ms. Foundation for Women, which was cofounded by Gloria Steinem and supports organizations advancing social, economic, and cultural change at the grassroots level.

"

I've grown up all of my life recognizing not everybody has a voice, not everybody's voice can be heard, and it's critical to have as many voices at the table as possible.

"

TERESA'S STORY

"To amplify the voices of women, and support movements, and trust women to know what will have the greatest impact in their communities is a very natural place for me to be.

On my very first day [at the Ms. Foundation], I walked into the office and saw these amazing pictures on the wall of the grantees. I realized right then and there that the work we were supporting was taking place on the ground throughout the United States.

So I decided I would do a listening tour. I'd spend my first year talking to our grantees, talking to friends of the Ms. Foundation, talking to people who knew Gloria and her work, and people who didn't know anything about us. I traveled about 53,000 miles and sat and listened to people tell me stories about why they were doing the work they were doing, and where their commitment was, and where they thought the work could be amplified, and what they thought we needed to be doing.

One of the key things I heard every time I asked a question around the definition of feminism was that people didn't define themselves as a feminist. They would say to me, 'This movement that you're talking about is really many movements. It's not just the women's movement but, rather, the movements that are affecting the lives of women. And we want to be part of it; we want to be part of making the world a better place.'

Each time I sat with different groups, I would hear slightly different things, but it all amounted to: 'You don't want me'—'you' meaning the women's movement or meaning the definition of feminism. The trans community would say to me, 'We're not feeling welcomed and safe.' Men were saying, 'You don't want us in this conversation.' Young women were saying, 'You don't understand, and you don't want us in this conversation.' Women of color were saying, 'You're not hearing what we have to say.'

What I heard was, 'We want a national diversified voice that's talking from a gender lens, that's talking from women's perspective, to challenge and question what's going on and to lend credibility to conversations.' So [at the Ms. Foundation] we're expanding the tent so everybody feels included in the conversation. We're challenging ourselves to think bigger and to be bolder in how we are looking at the intersections of everybody's lives and the work that we need to do to amplify, to empower, and to celebrate what's being done on the grassroots level so we can make it a true democracy that really values all of those voices."

TOOLS TO CHANGE THE WORLD

Recognize the intersections

"The lives of women are not monolithic. There are many complexities to the conversations, the successes, and the battles we still need to face and have an understanding of—where race, age, and gender intersect, where regionality comes into the conversation."

Talk about feminism

"We just need to own the word *feminism*, and we need to own the values and the definition behind it. We can't just assume everybody's going to feel comfortable with the terminology. But when we talk about the social, political, and economic equality of all genders, we're finding that actually invites people into the conversation."

Use your voice

"You have a voice and it needs to be heard. People don't need to agree with what you say. I've found that not everybody has been told that. Not everybody has been valued and not everybody has been supported in speaking up and speaking loudly and speaking often. And we need those voices."

Commit to your community

"My father was in service to this country, and my mother was my Girl Scout leader. I was in the Girl Scouts from when I was six years old, all the way until I finished a term as the president of the board of Girl Scouts of Connecticut. The idea was that we had a real commitment to our communities and that, once you are in community, you need to be present."

ADVICE TO KEEP GOING

Draw strength from the past to transform the future

"I grew up in an environment that wasn't racially diverse. So being the one and the only in a room was always something I anticipated. Being the first, however, was something I never anticipated. What I needed to do was recognize the shoulders I was standing on were those of women and those of people of color, and to make sure that I did them proud in the work they had done to lay the pavement for me to come forward.

I often talk about the fact that I stand in the shade of trees that I did not plant. And I walk down roads that I did not pave. And I drink from wells that I did not drill. My responsibility as a Black woman leading a national women's foundation is to make sure that I water the trees, and that I re-lay the pavement, and that I maintain the wells so that the generation that comes after me understands it didn't just happen that way."

SARAH McBRIDE

ADVANCE EQUALITY

Advocating for yourself can be the first step in changing systems to benefit others. Sarah McBride was a junior at American University, serving as student body president, when she used her social media platform to come out as a trans woman. Her goal: to humanize her experience and ward off potential bullying. Despite feeling her experience was mostly positive, it was the most difficult thing she had ever done. She realized she wanted to play a larger role in creating an accepting world for more trans people. The year after she came out, she was instrumental in getting her home state of Delaware to adopt its first gender identity nondiscrimination bill.

Sarah went on to work for the Human Rights Campaign and in 2015 made history—and a childhood dream come true—when she stood on the stage at the Democratic National Convention as the first transgender person to speak at a national political conference, during Hillary Clinton's own history-making nomination. In 2020, Sarah was elected to the Delaware state senate, becoming the highest-ranking openly trans official in the country, where she continues her fight for equality, justice, and fair policy.

"

Everyone should feel the fierce urgency of now.

"

SARAH'S STORY

"Most people in this country think that discrimination against LGBTQ people is clearly and explicitly illegal. And while we've made pretty significant progress, a majority of states and the federal government still haven't passed protections based on sexual orientation and gender identity in employment and housing in public spaces.

Delaware was one of those states that did not have explicit protections for transgender people when I came out in 2009. And I personally wanted to change that for myself and for other transgender people. So day in and day out during my senior year in college at American University I went up to Delaware when I was not in class to advocate to my state legislators the need to adopt the Gender Identity Nondiscrimination Act. For me it was really difficult because I had always done advocacy from the perspective of advocating for others. And this was in many ways my first experience directly advocating for myself.

I would come home on Tuesday nights, and my mom and I would drive down Wednesday and Thursday to the state legislature for about six months straight. We just literally camped out at the Legislative Hall, meeting with legislators in their offices but also in the halls, trying to catch them after meetings. It was an exhausting emotional experience. It was also a scary experience. I remember at one point a woman came up to me in the middle of the fight and asked, 'Sarah, have you had the surgery?' And I said, 'I'm sorry?' And she said, 'Have you had the surgery?' And I said, 'Ma'am, I don't think that's any of your business.' And she said, 'Well I'll tell you what, if I ever see you in a restroom. I'm going to …' And then she described assaulting me in the restroom. And I then reported that to the Capitol police officers. It should not be a natural by-product of advocating for your dignity to then be threatened with violence.

It was a scary experience, but at the end of the day it was inspiring for me to stand behind Governor Jack Markell, whom I had worked for and supported, and watch him sign into law that bill. To know that there would be generations of people in our state, people whom I will never know, who would benefit from that law. To know that our government, our society, and our community had just taken a step to affirm our dignity, to ensure equal protection under the law, and to make clear that we were part of the diversity of that state was a hopeful experience. And particularly so early on in my coming out journey, it convinced me that this work is worth it."

TOOLS TO CHANGE THE WORLD

Don't be afraid to feel vulnerable

"It took me a while to get to the point where I found the courage and the confidence in my own voice to be vulnerable and to share my own story; to talk about my own experiences and my own fears. Vulnerability transcends ideology, it transcends religion, race, gender, geography. Everyone understands what it feels like to be vulnerable at some point."

Be impatient

"Young people have a degree of impatience that I think all of us should feel. Everyone should feel the fierce urgency of now. Young people have passion behind their advocacy. I also think they're incredibly effective because young people are the ones who get to write the history books of tomorrow. They get to decide who was right and who was wrong in this moment."

Own your voice

"Everyone understands what it feels like to be scared or fearful. For me it was a journey through that process of finding my own voice, of finding my own story, and of finally gaining confidence in the importance of sharing my experience."

Use your platform

"I knew that my coming out would be something that people would talk about. I felt like I had a responsibility as student body president to use what little platform I had to try to educate people a little bit more about what it's like to be transgender and about my own experience; to try to demonstrate that behind this conversation are real people who love and laugh, hope and fear, dream and cry just like everyone else."

ADVICE TO KEEP GOING

"You are the best expert on who you are and what you need. And you are the best expert on how you will feel safe. You are the best expert on your well-being. And there is no one-size-fits-all in these journeys. There's no one narrative, there's no one way to be you. Do what you need to do to be safe, to be healthy. And in your advocacy, there's no wrong way to be you. Don't try to feel like you need to conform your narrative or your story to what you think is the most palatable or the most dramatic. Just allow yourself to be authentic because people will respond. But take care of yourself."

"

There's no one narrative, there's no one way to be you. Do what you need to do to be safe, to be healthy.

"

RESHMA SAUJANI

EMBRACE IMPOSSIBLE

It's worth trying something new, even if you know you might fail, because the experience itself can be transformative. In 2009, Reshma Saujani was the first Indian American woman to run for the US House of Representatives. She went up against a decades-long incumbent, and while she lost the race, she won the confidence to take on other big challenges. During school visits on the campaign trail, Reshma learned about the growing gender gap in computer science. In response, she founded the nonprofit Girls Who Code to shift the culture of the tech industry and bring more girls into computer programming. She refers to herself as a "recovering perfectionist," and her podcast, book, and website, *Brave, Not Perfect*, encourage more failure and less fear. Undaunted by the challenges of systemic change, she's now leading the call for a Marshall Plan for Moms and has written a book on how to transform the American workplace called *Pay Up*. Through these avenues and others, she advocates for women's unseen and unpaid work and is advancing a policy change platform for basic income, affordable childcare, pay equity, and parental leave.

"

Go do the thing that you thought you were bad at.

"

RESHMA'S STORY

Generations of my family have lived in Africa. My parents came to the United States as refugees from Uganda, expelled in 1973 by the dictator Idi Amin. They lost everything. They were big believers in the American dream: You come here, you educate your children, they get really high-paying jobs, and they help pay the mortgage. And so for them, I was doing that. I was working as a lawyer in finance, making more money than they had ever seen in their whole lives. But I think they realized how miserable I was. The moment when I called my dad and said, 'Look, I'm running for office,' I think he had one word: 'Finally.'

I don't think I knew that the odds were against me. I thought I could shake every hand and meet every voter and convince the world they should vote for me. I mean, ignorance is bliss, right? Sometimes you don't know any better, and it was a really brave moment for me. For so long in my life and my career, I was just doing everything right. I went to Yale Law School because I felt like that would help open doors. Worked in finance because that's what all the kids were doing then. Worked for a law firm. Made all these choices based on what I thought I should do to preserve optionality and build my résumé. And through all of it, I was miserable.

I always wanted to do public service and social service, and I was so off my path. At age thirty-three I took a bold step. I quit my job, and I ran for Congress in a Democratic primary against an eighteen-year incumbent. I had no idea what I was doing. I had immigrant parents who couldn't tell me how to build a campaign, how to raise money, or what to do when I got on television. Nobody in my world and in my life could direct me. We all kind of just figured it out.

I think having such a colossal loss at age thirty-three freed me up to take other risks in my life. Just losing like that and losing so big and being so humiliated was the best thing that ever happened to me."

TOOLS TO CHANGE THE WORLD

Don't be afraid to fail

"Why are women afraid of failure? Well, it's because they've been taught to be perfect. What we've seen is that women gravitate toward the things we think we're good at, and stay away from the things we think we're bad at. Whereas men are constantly taking risks and are rewarded for it. So my whole thing is, how do we get girls and women to be comfortable with imperfection at all ages?"

Learn new skills

"Technology is going to be a part of everything we do. Because of that perfection thing, if we're not comfortable with a topic, we're going to stay away from it. So we might have a great business idea, but we may be afraid to start our company because we're afraid to converse with engineers because we think that they're going to have some knowledge we don't have. Even being able to know enough that you can talk with a technical person is really important."

Shape the future through technology

"Coding in the 21st century is going to be a basic skill set like reading and writing. Jobs in computer science are solving the problems of today and tomorrow, whether it's cancer or climate change, or they're building the next-generation companies like Instagram, Twitter, or Facebook. If you don't have women as part of this growth, you're simply missing out."

Solve problems that interest you

"Studies show that 74 percent of girls want to pick a profession that's about changing the world. I think that girls intuitively are problem solvers, community oriented, and change agents. I think we'll see that, as women get more access to technical skills, they are going to use those skills to solve problems in their communities and the world."

Focus on culture change

"The reality is, today in America, tween girls decide what's cool and what's not cool. So we're thinking about interesting, provocative ways to get girls interested in coding; to shape culture and to tell the media, 'We're going to pay attention to what is on television shows and in movies. And we're going to make sure that girls are represented. Because you cannot be what you cannot see.'"

ADVICE TO KEEP GOING

Don't overthink it

"Sometimes we overthink things. With Girls Who Code, if I had overthought it, if that idea didn't come to me at a certain moment in time where I'd been through so much, I don't think I ever would have done it. People will say to me, 'I have this idea' and I'm like, 'Great. Just try it. Just start it.'"

SHANNON WATTS

TURN OUTRAGE INTO ACTION

You can apply the skills you have to the transformational change you want to make. In the wake of the mass shooting at Sandy Hook Elementary School in 2012, Shannon Watts started a conversation on social media that turned into a grassroots movement, which ultimately became the organization she now leads, Moms Demand Action for Gun Sense in America.

As more mothers (many of them gun owners) joined in, they brought their skills to the table. In between work commitments and during their children's naps, these moms organized, showed up at lawmakers' offices, and demanded safer gun laws. Together they have made a dent in the NRA's power. Now many of those same women are taking what they learned as activists and running for office—and winning at all levels, from city council to Congress. Shannon continues to lead Moms Demand Action and is on the advisory board of Emerge America. She chronicles her journey in her book, *Fight Like a Mother: How a Grassroots Movement Took on the Gun Lobby and Why Women Will Change the World.*

SHANNON'S STORY

"The day the news started to come in over my television, I remember I was folding huge piles of laundry. I have five kids. I was in Indiana. I'd been a stay-at-home mom for about five years, taking a break from my career in corporate communications because my kids were at that age where you don't really want them home alone.

The news was coming in that there had been a horrific tragedy in Newtown, Connecticut. I can remember just sort of saying to the universe, 'Please don't let this be as bad as it seems.' And what started to unfold was really unfathomable—that twenty children and six educators could be slaughtered in the sanctity of an elementary school is even today too much to bear.

I was, like every American, devastated. But then pundits started coming on my television, saying the solution was more guns. As if 400 million guns in the hands of civilians just wasn't quite cutting it. I didn't know a thing about organizing or gun policy or gun laws. I just knew that was not true. So I went online and thought, *Okay. I'm going to join something like Mothers Against Drunk Driving for gun safety—surely that exists*. And I couldn't find anything. I found mostly male-run think tanks in Washington, DC. I found some one-off state organizations, again mostly run by men, and I thought, 'Well, what can I do from here?' I really wanted to be part of this grassroots army of women to fight on this issue.

So I thought, *I'll start a Facebook page and just have that conversation*. I'm not really sure why I thought it would turn into a conversation because I had seventy-five Facebook friends and I didn't even have an active Twitter handle. But it was like lightning in a bottle, where all these Type A women from across the country started Googling my personal information and calling me and texting me and sending emails and saying, 'I want to do this where I live.' They had the same idea that day, that it was time to get off the sidelines.

Moms are the majority of the public. Our votes are the majority of the voting electorate, but also our spending power. We make 80 percent of the spending decisions for our families, so those are the levers of power that we're pulling. We couldn't be a silent majority anymore. And it's much like any other social issue in this country: it doesn't start in Congress, it ends in Congress. We had to build political power in a movement that could go toe to toe with the gun lobby. Six and a half years later, we're now larger than the NRA."

TOOLS TO CHANGE THE WORLD

Get out of your bubble

"As a white suburban mom, I was living in a bubble, not realizing the gun violence that occurs every day in this country and that women of color in particular have been fighting these battles for decades, and they've been invisible. It's so important that we partner with different organizations because it's the only way we address this issue. We all have to work together."

Investigate systemic cause and effect

"Intersectionality is important to the issue of gun violence. We talk about how it impacts women's lives, how it impacts communities of color, trans Americans, the LGBTQ community, all of it. We have to look at what the roots of gun violence are and bring all those communities in to help address it."

Push your cause to be a priority

"These shootings are completely preventable and senseless. Our Moms Demand Action volunteers show up not just at gun bill hearings but town halls and debates. We show up everywhere in our red T-shirts to make sure that the issue of gun sense is front and center."

Propel change at the polls

"We know when women go to the polls they vote on this issue and that when they run for office and win, they legislate on this issue. So all of it is about turbocharging this effort and speeding it up so that we can start to make real progress."

Empower with data

"[Gun regulation] can be a polarizing conversation. But when you are discussing it in a very rational, research-based way, it's easier. For so long gun lobbyists have spread misinformation that has become part of the zeitgeist. And when you go in and say, 'Actually this is the case, this is the situation,' it's much easier because it's not as emotion driven."

"

You're not going to win every battle, but you're going to learn enough to win the next one.

"

ADVICE TO KEEP GOING

"You're not going to have easy wins overnight. You're just not. It is going to be a marathon, not a sprint. There are going to be many losses along the way. And it's so important that you learn when you lose. Because you're not going to win every battle, but you're going to learn enough to win the next one and ultimately the war. That's the big-picture way to look at it."

ANNE-MARIE SLAUGHTER

DON'T SETTLE FOR HALFWAY

Personal experience can drive societal transformation. In 2012, Anne-Marie Slaughter left a high-profile role as the first female director of policy planning for the US Department of State to make more time for her sons. She then wrote a piece about this decision for the *Atlantic*, titled "Why Women Still Can't Have It All." It sparked considerable debate and became one of the most-read pieces in the magazine's history.

Today, Anne-Marie is president and CEO of the think and action tank New America. She is also professor emerita at Princeton University, where she was the Dean of the School of Public and International Affairs. Prior to that she was professor of international, foreign, and comparative law at Harvard Law School. *Foreign Policy* magazine included her four times on their annual list of the Top 100 Global Thinkers. She has written and edited eight books including her follow up to the *Atlantic* piece, *Unfinished Business: Women, Men, Work, Family*, which outlines her belief that the only way to achieve an equal society is to prioritize policies and practices that value caregiving as highly as breadwinning.

> **"**
>
> # You can't change women's roles and say, 'Okay, now you can be breadwinners,' but still expect them to entirely be caregivers. That's a halfway revolution.
>
> **"**

ANNE-MARIE'S STORY

"I had every advantage in the world. I had a husband who was the lead parent at home. I had money. I had the ability to shape my life as much as anybody does. And yet when I went to Washington, DC, and was commuting, I had a teenage son who really needed all hands on deck, and I hit a tipping point. I took two years out initially because my kid really needed both my husband and me. And then another two where I wanted to be home because it would be the last four years that both my kids would be home.

No matter how carefully you plan, things don't go as planned. You can have a child with special needs, or you can have a divorce, or you can have a parent move away, or you have to move. When you hit that tipping point, we have to create support. And, critically, we have to understand that, just because you may work differently or have stopped working to take care of whatever the problem was, you're still really smart, talented, educated, and experienced.

It's kind of extraordinary that there's this idea that by taking time to take care of other people—which clearly from a social point of view is necessary, and from an economic and even national security point of view, investing in kids is critical to our future—is some kind of moral and intellectual deficit, as if people who have done that have lost IQ points. Their previous experience was for nothing. They didn't get any valuable experience caregiving. It simply makes no sense.

A lot of women, we say they 'opted out,' but actually they were shut out, because if you talk to women who are at home, the majority will tell you—and I'm drawing on sociological research here—that they wanted to stay in the workforce but wanted to work three days a week. Or they wanted to work from home one day a week. Or they wanted flexible hours, and their employers wouldn't let them. So it was full time or out. The starting point is that we should be able to keep them in the workforce. And second, if they do want to be out beyond maternity leave, then there should be on-ramps to get them back in. And societies that won't let women do that are societies that are missing out on their talent."

TOOLS TO CHANGE THE WORLD

Value caregiving as much as breadwinning

"The United States values competition, but we devalue care. And you can't run a competitive economy without giving people the ability to care for each other. It won't work. If you don't pay for it or provide it or make it accessible, then you burn people out and they can't be productive, and ultimately the society tips over."

Reshape responsibilities

"Men's roles really have to change. They have to be caregivers as well as breadwinners. Men are really missing out on one of life's greatest pleasures and activities: the sense of purpose and meaning and love that you have in caring for others, even when it's hard and boring. Men need to have the same range of choices and roles that we now think women should have."

Debate with an open mind

"When you are debating something with someone, if your view is 'I'm right and you need to change your view,' that becomes very adversarial. So when I'm in a debate, I try to go with an open mind, accepting that my own views are likely to change. And then, if my views change, you think, 'Well, this is a real debate. I just changed your mind.' And you hear me differently."

ADVICE TO KEEP GOING

Interval train

"We need to elongate the arc of a successful career. Think about a career as interval training, like athletes who go hard and slow down, and go hard again and slow down. That's how they get peak performance. Similarly, over a lifetime, why can't we think of men and women as having periods where they go hard and then periods where they want other things in their lives? A woman who's sixty or fifty-five still has ten to fifteen, even twenty years of good working life, although perhaps part time. Why not say, 'You actually can do both if we can change social and economic attitudes,' and that way both women and men would have better lives and still could reach the top."

A'SHANTI GHOLAR

TRANSFORM POLITICAL LEADERSHIP

When you hold political office, you hold power. And even though women make up 51 percent of the population, by most estimates it could be 100 years until we have gender parity in elected offices, with an even longer road for Black, Brown, Asian, and Indigenous women. In her role as president of Emerge, A'shanti Gholar is working to change this traditional power structure. As founder of The Brown Girls Guide to Politics website and podcast, she provides a network and source of advice for women of color, whether they already hold political office or are exploring it.

She has worked for the Democratic National Committee; as a political appointee in the Obama Administration at the US Department of Labor; and as the Director of Public Engagement for the 2012 Democratic National Convention Committee in Charlotte, North Carolina.

At Emerge, A'shanti leads the charge to recruit and train Democratic women to run for office and win at every level of government. She has also worked as an organizer and sees many opportunities for women to affect laws and policy. A'shanti focuses on equipping women to overcome obstacles, rise up, and lead.

"

So many women, especially women of color, are so great at getting other people elected, but I want us to see our name on the ballot; to be able to go into the voting booth and vote for ourselves.

"

A'SHANTI'S STORY

"I grew up in Las Vegas, Nevada. I was watching TV one day with my mom, and she left the room, and I changed the channel and discovered C-SPAN. I saw all of these people arguing and fighting about making the country better, and that's when I developed my love of politics. But I didn't see a lot of people that look like me, a lot of women of color.

When I was in high school, I had that amazing government teacher you hear about. She was well connected and had the candidates for a statewide senate race come into our classroom. One of the candidates I loved; I enjoyed everything that he said, his stances on the issues. The other candidate, I had an issue with the fact that he voted against raising the minimum wage. For me it was very important because I had lots of friends that worked part-time jobs, either to make extra money to support being a teenager or to bring extra money home. And I thought they should make more money and that people in general should make more money. I asked the candidate why he voted against raising the minimum wage. He said he didn't. I said, 'Yes you did. I can look up your votes.' And he argued with me, just saying that he didn't.

After the class he called my government teacher and said to her, 'She was right. I didn't vote to raise it. I just didn't like the fact that she called me out.' And it absolutely infuriated me. I thought, *Well, is it because I'm a girl? Is it because I can't vote? I'm young?* All of those things were very true. But even though I was young, and I couldn't vote, and I was a girl, I could volunteer. So every moment that I had to spare I volunteered for his opponent, and his opponent ended up winning that race by less than 500 votes.

When my government teacher told me he had called, I was just all, 'Lord, I'm in so much trouble now 'cause I was arguing with this man.' But she actually said she was really proud of me for standing up and pushing back, and she told the whole class the next day how he had called and apologized.

I never knew what political parties she was involved in, but when I ran for secretary of the Nevada State Democratic Party, my teacher was there at the convention, and she said, 'I saw your name and that you were running, and I had to show up and support you, and I still tell my students about what you did to this day.'"

TOOLS TO CHANGE THE WORLD

Be your own perfect candidate

"The only candidate who's going to 100 percent agree with you on any issue is you, literally, so you need to be running for office. If you want the perfect candidate, you need to be running, challenging people, and making the change. You have to take your own advice, get out there and get comfortable, be the one to do what you really love, and step up in this space."

Know your why, your what, and your how

"One of the first things I ask women all the time is, 'Why are you running?' You have to have your why. The best elected officials I see are those who start off as activists. Those who had something important in their community that they wanted to change. And then they ran for office themselves, and they learned how to make the system work for the things they wanted to do."

Embrace learning

"As women, we put all of this pressure on ourselves, but it is that thinking that makes really great candidates. We put out amazing platforms that reflect the community because we're going around learning. We're not expecting that we know everything about every single issue. We go to the experts."

Get in the room

"Even when we talk about women's issues, we still need to realize these are family issues, these are community issues, these are 'everyone' issues. And we need women from different backgrounds—socioeconomic, racial, ethnic—to be helping draft those laws because when we're not helping draft them, then they have a very negative impact on us when they're implemented."

Reconsider what it means to represent

"For women of color, we wake up every day and we're playing in a system that was not built for us, that never imagined our participation. Politics was made for white land-owning men. We still have to realize that our elected officials need to look like the people in this country. We need to make sure we're not thinking that people of color can only represent people of color. This is such an antiquated idea. We have to get out of that mindset. We are capable of doing a lot more for entire communities."

Speak up for others

"When it comes to the racism, the sexism, the homophobia, all of these things that exist, we, as those people experiencing it, cannot be the ones constantly calling it out. We need white people to be the ones saying, 'Hey, this is not right. I see what is happening. Do you see what is happening?'"

"

Even though you may not be feeling that you are seen and heard, know that there are other women that do see you and value you.

"

ADVICE TO KEEP GOING

"For the young women who are coming up in politics, I want them to know that there are women working in this space to make it better for them. And that is something that my friends and I really concentrate on. After we leave an organization or role in a company, we always ask ourselves, 'Have I made this better for the young women of color who are coming after me?' And we always want that answer to be 'Yes.'"

SHARE

CELEBRATE, GATHER, AND GROW

Share your ideas. Share your successes. Share your failures. And share your joy! Change is never done, so take time to honor your impact and reflect as you go. Every time you share your story, you build hope, community, and momentum. Your successes motivate more people to join you. Your obstacles guide the next person on their own journey.

The mighty women in this chapter speak their truth, lead with love, and seek out perspectives different from their own. They rely on rest, reflection, and close relationships to keep going . . . and to dream big once again.

JOAN BLADES

CROSS THE DIVIDE

While it's easy to spend time with people who agree with us, Joan Blades believes real progress comes from conversations with people who don't. She is a domestic peace builder, mediator, entrepreneur, and movement organizer. Her career includes cofounding Berkeley Systems (best known for the flying toaster screen saver and popular 1990s game *You Don't Know Jack*); cofounding MoveOn, a progressive advocacy group that laid the groundwork for the future of digital organizing; and cofounding MomsRising, a grassroots organization that advocates for paid family leave, maternal health, and other family-friendly policies. In 2010, Joan cofounded Living Room Conversations to bring members of the left and right sides of the political spectrum into civil discourse to solve urgent public policy problems and identify shared values.

> ## Listening is way more powerful than we ever think it is.

JOAN'S STORY

"People are increasingly homogenous in the groups they hang out with. When we talk to our friends we're told similar beliefs, and it causes us to hold those beliefs even more strongly and push us farther in whatever direction we're already leaning. This is a real problem when it comes to being able to work collaboratively.

We have to start having real, meaningful engagement with each other. And in fact, there's a whole lot more shared common ground than we're focusing on. There are opportunities for us to work together, and we've worked ourselves into such divisive corners that we don't see them.

I got into this originally because I wanted to know, back in 2004, why conservatives weren't concerned about climate change. I mean, we all want the future to be good for future generations. I was able to sit down with conservative leadership on the right and have a good conversation at that time. And there was some curiosity and interest. Now, years later, it is clear that the line between left and right is more rigid and more impenetrable.

Living Room Conversations are a very intentional way to allow people to dissipate those lines so they can start to have enough of a relationship to hear each other. We generally don't change dramatically in one conversation, but we do open up, and I have seen people change over time. I certainly have changed because of the relationships I have with friends that have very different viewpoints than I do."

TOOLS TO CHANGE THE WORLD

Engage with respect

"I'm really uncomfortable with conflict where people are abusing each other. I hate that. But I'm very comfortable with conflict where people are expressing their differences and actually doing so in a respectful manner."

Expand your connection

"There are a lot of people I know that hold very, very different beliefs than I do. It's actually more interesting and more fun to look for the things we agree on, and we can work on, than focusing on the things we disagree on that make us angry. And then I think there's a strong possibility that we'll see more things we can work on together and agree on. We may never get to complete consensus, but we would be living in a much kinder, stronger, more robust community and country if we started doing this."

Listen with care

"Science tells us that emotion trumps logic in the vast majority of our decision-making. So if we don't have that heart piece woven into what we're teaching, we're missing the most important part. Because once I like you, I listen to you in a completely different way."

Don't try to persuade

"People think that it's about persuading leaders that X or Y is important. It's not. The most effective way to persuade someone is to not try to persuade them of anything. It's about working together in a manner where you've got everyone's best ideas in the room, and you've got the agility to stop doing what's not working, do more of what's working, and work with each other because that's the only way we're going to come up with a reasonable solution."

ADVICE TO KEEP GOING

"When I sit down with my circle of conservative friends, I see wonderful people that are caring and intelligent and all the things you want in a friend. And I learn from them why they have the viewpoint they do. Pretty often we can find ways to navigate some really important issues. I have to have faith that, with a good relationship, more will become possible and we'll each see each other in a more full way."

"

With a good relationship, more will become possible.

"

EMILY LADAU

BREAK DOWN BARRIERS

Emily Ladau believes there is power in talking openly about your experiences. Emily has Larsen syndrome, a rare genetic joint and muscle disorder she inherited from her mom, who has it too. She was born in 1991, the year after the passage of the Americans with Disabilities Act. And while this major law guaranteed people with disabilities the same opportunities as everyone else, its intent has not yet been fully realized. Emily believes this is both because of ableist attitudes and a lack of systemic change. She is on a mission to break down barriers to progress for disability rights by sharing her own story and helping others do the same on their own terms. She jokes that she is a "professional disabled person," but her work is serious. She has won a number of awards for her activism, consults on communications and social media strategy for multiple disability-related organizations and initiatives, and cohosts a podcast called *The Accessible Stall*. Her first book is *Demystifying Disability: What to Know, What to Say, and How to Be an Ally*. Her first act of activism was to appear on the PBS children's show *Sesame Street*.

"

It is by sharing our stories and making the disability experience accessible to the world that we will reach a world that is accessible to the disability community.

"

EMILY'S STORY

"I'm very, very passionate about storytelling, not just my own story, but finding ways to amplify as many stories as I possibly can. It wasn't until I was ten that I started to understand that my story actually matters to people, and I wasn't just some kind of object of fascination. I had the opportunity to appear on several episodes of *Sesame Street*, which came to be because I went to a summer camp for kids with disabilities. That was really the only place during the year where I would see myself reflected back at myself. The rest of the year, the only example of an apparent disability I saw on a regular basis was my mother. The camp got a phone call and they said, 'Hey, we're looking for kids to try out for a role on *Sesame Street*. Do you have anyone?'

I was loud and precocious and probably annoying. And they said, 'Yeah, we've got someone who never stops talking!' So I auditioned for the role and got the part. In hindsight, this was the moment when I realized my voice was actually capable of making a difference in how people perceive disability, essentially just by being myself. That was a really powerful pivot point, and looking back on it, I think it is the reason for where I am today.

Following my time on *Sesame Street*, I would talk about my disability if I felt like it was convenient or if I felt like the moment was right. But beyond that, the best thing you could possibly say to me was, 'Oh, I forgot that you use a wheelchair' or 'I don't think of you as disabled.' I just wanted to hide this very apparent thing about myself and not call attention to it.

It wasn't until college when I started to wake up to the fact that there was no reason for me to be trying to hide something. First of all, I couldn't hide anyway. And second of all, I shouldn't have to hide. Midway through college, I had what I call a quarter-life crisis, where I just completely cracked. And I was like, 'I need to be a disability advocate. I don't know what that means, but I'm going to do it.' My parents, being the beautiful humans that they are, were like, 'We have no idea what you're saying. We don't know how you're going to make money, but we love you. So go for it.'

I'm doing what I can to take the experience of disability and make it more accessible to people and more understandable and relatable in the hopes that we can have bigger conversations about it because we'll be less afraid of saying the wrong thing or doing the wrong thing. And we'll be able to show up as we are and hopefully learn better, and then know better, and then do better."

TOOLS TO CHANGE THE WORLD

Talk about disability

"I always say that disabled people are on the margins of marginalization because, even in conversations about marginalized groups, we don't talk about disability. When we start to recognize that disability is not this niche issue or identity—actually more than a billion disabled people exist around the world—you start to understand it's something that cuts across every identity. We need to be talking about it or we're leaving people behind."

Connect at an individual level

"I'm the type of person who is less about broad, sweeping changes and more about meeting people where they're at—connecting on an individual level in the hopes that one conversation or one person reading my book might have a ripple effect outward. To me it is so much more powerful to bridge gaps in that small way than to try to take this 30,000-foot view of needing to change everything all at once."

Seek small wins

"Combating ableism begins by taking a look around the environments you're in and asking what you're doing to make them inclusive and accessible. Whether it is going to a shop that you frequent and saying, 'Hey, it would be so great if you could put a ramp in,' or if you are planning an event, ensuring there's going to be captioning so everybody can understand what's being said. When we begin to make these small changes and create environments that are more meaningfully inclusive, we can start to dismantle how pervasive ableism really is."

Break the ice with storytelling

"If I want someone to understand my experiences, I want them to learn those experiences from me whenever possible. I don't want them to make assumptions. I don't want them to make snap judgments. I would much rather share a part of my story or point them to someone else who is sharing their story so that they can learn directly from people who have lived experience. And it's from this storytelling that I think we will begin to break a lot of the ice that exists between nondisabled people and disabled people."

Destigmatize "disabled"

"I try to caution people against the use of euphemisms like 'special needs' or 'differently abled.' That being said, if someone who has a disability chooses to use those terms for themselves, I respect that. What it comes down to is honoring each person's preference where you can, but on the whole not being afraid of the word *disability*. That's not a bad word. It's a word. It describes who I am. And the only reason we see it as dehumanizing is because we've attached that connotation to it, which means that we also have the power to remove it."

"

I am trying really, really hard to make more time for myself intentionally.

"

ADVICE TO KEEP GOING

"I used to keep a very odd sleep schedule, and I would always be waking up late and rushing to all of my meetings for the day. I finally realized if I just wake up at the same time every single morning, give myself some time to eat something, to exercise, to move my body in a way that feels good, to start my day by putting myself first, that it would really make a difference in the tone of my day. I know I sound like some kind of women's health magazine or something. I don't mean to; I'm not one of those people. But it really has made a difference for me."

RACHEL SIMMONS

SHARE YOUR FAILURES

We live in a culture that tells girls they can do anything, expects them to be everything, and stigmatizes them for achieving too much. To confront this toxic concoction, Rachel Simmons, an internationally recognized researcher and educator, works with girls and women to value emotional health over external markers of success and to not trade self-worth and wellness in pursuit of achievement. She is the author of *Odd Girl Out*, *Enough as She Is*, and several other books. She is also the cofounder of Girls Leadership, an organization that teaches girls how to be authentic, assertive, and resilient. Rachel was one of the first to call out the increasing number of young American women and girls suffering from depression, anxiety, and exhaustion in the early 2000s. As a driven high performer herself, she knew the signs. She ultimately survived by discovering the power of sharing her story.

>"
The act of telling your story can be transformative.
"

RACHEL'S STORY

"I was so worried about what would happen if people knew my real backstory.

In a very concerted effort to be this amazing overachiever person, I applied for the Rhodes Scholarship and won a free ride to Oxford University. At the time, I'd been working for the mayor of New York and then had transitioned to working for Chuck Schumer, who was in his first campaign for the Senate. I had a kind of storied young career out of college, and the Rhodes felt like the capstone of all of that.

So off I went to Oxford, and pretty quickly after arriving I felt this pit in my stomach, like 'this is not for me.' First of all, it gets dark at four o'clock in the afternoon. And I was a lesbian in a not super lesbian-friendly environment. I wanted to study feminist political theory, so what was I doing in a place where everything that we read was by people who were very dead and very white? The other Rhodes Scholars were not like me in the sense that they didn't want to go to Amsterdam and smoke pot like I did. I was like, 'We're in Europe! Let's do this!' And they were like, 'I'm going to have a confirmation hearing in ten years.' So there's a lot that didn't work.

Ultimately, I got very depressed. I came to understand that my whole life and self-esteem had been defined by my accomplishments. And at the same time, so obsessed had I become with these accomplishments that I really disconnected from what I cared about. After much agonizing and ruminating and a lot of therapy and medication, I ultimately dropped out of Oxford, which became a source of great shame. And I hid this for a long time from public view.

I was told by the president of my college that I had embarrassed the college, having only been the second Rhodes Scholar ever in the college's history. It was an awful, demoralizing time. I ended up eventually writing my first book, *Odd Girl Out*. In the process I was invited to work at a girls' leadership summer camp in Washington, DC, through the Sidwell Friends School, which is a Quaker school in Washington. Something inside me began to take hold in a more passionate way than I'd ever felt. And I rolled with it.

I started working with teenagers at Oprah [Winfrey]'s Leadership Academy for Girls right outside of Johannesburg, a very high-achieving school, and decided one day to talk to them about what had happened in Oxford. The looks on their faces when I was telling them about being on this achievement treadmill, losing touch with myself, being consistently unable to handle failure, it was like they lit up because they understood. I was giving a language to something they had been experiencing. So that was my 'aha' moment. I did need to be in another hemisphere from the one in which I currently live in order to share it. It was really liberating. The act of telling your story can be transformative. And that's really what I was doing."

TOOLS TO CHANGE THE WORLD

Connect to something bigger

"More and more girls and women are raising their voices around political change. We're not seeing the emphasis on achievement; we're seeing more of an emphasis on making a difference and changing the culture. That's really healthy for girls because it's connecting them to something bigger than themselves. I think where girls are in trouble is when they believe that achieving equality is more about individual success than being part of something bigger than they are."

Talk about mistakes

"Make a point of sharing your mistakes regularly with your kids. To be able to say, 'I'm not perfect. I have survived mistake-making, and I'm still the same awesome person and good parent that you always thought I was.' That's very, very important for girls to have regular contact with."

Call out broken systems

"I really advise parents to make sure your kid knows that you know their struggle is not their fault. This is not about one child's inability to keep up with the stress. This is a broken, toxic culture around success and achievement. Talk about the guardrails that are going to help you achieve in the ways you want to without giving up your wellness or your self-worth. What that's going to look like for a high school student is, 'Maybe I'm going to take three classes instead of five this year. Maybe I need a mental health day to stay home from school and just stare into space for the day.'"

Confront worst-case scenarios

"When I'm facing down an uncertain situation, I ask myself, 'What is the worst that could happen?' If you constantly imagine the worst possible outcome or tell yourself that the worst thing is going to happen or has happened, that digs a trench in your brain. It's going to affect your confidence; it's going to affect your risk-taking ability. So you actually have to say, 'Wait, what's the real worst that could happen?' And then secondly, can you live with that?"

"

If we don't experience gratitude for what we have, we're always looking down the road for what's next.

"

ADVICE TO KEEP GOING

"Perfectionism in part comes from a lack of self-compassion, this 'girl power' obsession and sense that you have to be all that you can be all the time and be everything to everyone—which no one can. There's a process, there's a journey. It's not always about the polished finish. It's about the minimum benefit that you got from doing something. It's about trying things where you know you might fail. We all have to commit ourselves to that every day. When you can pause and have gratitude for the things that did go well, there's a real palliative effect to that."

CARRIE GOLDBERG

GALVANIZE CHANGE

The #MeToo movement was founded by activist Tarana Burke in 2006 to provide support and healing to other survivors of sexual assault. In 2017, in the wake of accusations against media mogul Harvey Weinstein, #MeToo became a hashtag used more than nineteen million times on Twitter by women across the world emboldened to speak out about sexual harassment and assault in their own work and personal lives. This outpouring exposed the scale of the problem and was a powerful catalyst for change. Attorney Carrie Goldberg, who represented one of Weinstein's accusers, has made it her life's goal to get justice and restore safety and privacy for victims of sexual assault, antiabortion harassment, stalking, and other egregious acts. She advocates for laws that criminalize revenge porn and goes after Title IX violations. She is also committed to changing laws that protect websites and big tech from liability for the conduct of their users. In her book, *Nobody's Victim: Fighting Psychos, Stalkers, Pervs, and Trolls*, she shares her own experience as the target of revenge porn and her extraordinary work to "transform clients from victims into warriors."

CARRIE'S STORY

"I had met somebody on the internet who knocked me off my feet. After a couple of months it became a very frightening relationship, which I ended. And by ending it, it started a tsunami of stalking and absolutely unrelenting amounts of contact from him. Hundreds, if not thousands of text messages and phone calls, and him trying to break in to my apartment, and showing up at work, and contacting dozens of my friends and family, spreading vicious rumors about me. It went on and on. I had to move. I had to start working from a different location.

One of the things he was also doing was sending me naked pictures and videos of myself, telling me—I was already a lawyer at the time—that judges and my colleagues had been blind-copied on these emails. So almost immediately I reported it to the police. And the police said, 'We can investigate, but you're probably going to be better off if you go and get a family court order of protection.'

Which I did go and do. There was this sobering eureka moment where I was speaking to the judge, and I was requesting that he grant me an order that not only required my offender to stay away from me and not contact me at home or work, but that also required the offender to stop threatening and harassing me online—to not post anything else, not contact my family, and not send nude videos and pictures to anybody.

The judge looked at me and said, 'You know, I suggest you get a lawyer. I know you are one, but I suggest you get one because you've got a First Amendment problem.' Everything went silent. And I was like, 'What the judge is saying is that it's freedom of speech for this total crazy man to express himself by sending pictures of my genitals around.'

And after a lot of further hell, I ultimately succeeded in getting my restraining order, and my life just looked nothing like it had before. I decided I was going to quit my job and spend the rest of my life becoming for others the lawyer that I really needed.

I started the firm in January 2014, just a few short months after I got my restraining order. I'm happy to say that we have helped hundreds of people. We've gotten thousands of videos and images removed from the internet. We've gotten dozens of restraining orders. We've initiated some really great cases against tech companies whose platforms facilitate harassment and stalking. And I've helped with creating and writing and advocating for a lot of state laws relating to sextortion and revenge porn.

So it ended up that the worst thing that ever happened to me became something I'm completely grateful for, and that my staff and I have been able to use to help a lot more people."

TOOLS TO CHANGE THE WORLD

Keep speaking out

"We need to believe people who've been abused by somebody powerful. We need to remember it's not uncommon for powerful people to abuse and sexually harass. And we have to keep encouraging people to speak out because the stories are what's going to galvanize social change."

Don't stand by

"The people who are powerful live and die by their reputation. And people with less power have a hand in creating reputations. So if there's buzz about somebody abusing their power, you can't just say, 'Oh, that's just Harvey.' You have to say, 'That power-mongering is unacceptable.' We need to rely on our standards—whether at school, work, or in the public square—to hold that person accountable."

"

Keep encouraging people to speak out because the stories are what's going to galvanize social change.

"

Demand corporate transparency

"As a society, we need to ostracize those who abuse power. We should stop investing in companies run by those who harass. Investors in companies should demand full transparency about staff complaints and sexual harassment settlements, and we should boycott products where companies are guilty of fostering harassing environments."

Get out the truth

"Lawsuits are the ultimate equalizer. They are public and hold people accountable by getting justice for the injured person and by exposing the injuring person. They are a really important way to get out the truth. People have to make sworn statements on the record, which can be used by other victims. One victim might sue, and suddenly more and more will read about it and realize there are other people that this happened to."

Support sex ed and consent ed in school

"Consent education needs to start at a very, very young age. This isn't about teaching our daughters not to send a naked picture or not to get raped. It needs to be expressed to the boys. And schools are the best place to do that. There needs to be a budget for this stuff."

ADVICE TO KEEP GOING

Stay focused on the outcome

"I talk to my clients about the idea of post-traumatic growth. In these situations where you're under incredible stress, it's very normal to go to places of comfort. That can be alcohol, drugs, or sex. I don't recommend that because, especially when you're in a moment of vulnerability, it can really get out of hand. It's okay to feel sorry for yourself and to have emotional collapses now and then, but the misery a person feels during their time of crisis is temporary. When they get to the other side of their crisis, they're going to be confident in themselves that they made a series of good decisions that led them to this outcome. And they're going to feel more resilient and empowered, and suddenly things that they may have been scared of aren't frightening anymore."

PAOLA GIANTURCO
AND ALEX SANGSTER

SHINE A LIGHT

There are girls all around the globe addressing tough issues in their communities no young person should have to deal with— but often must—by virtue of where and when they were born. Issues like child marriage, access to education, air pollution, and freedom of expression. Award-winning photojournalist Paola Gianturco and her then ten-year-old granddaughter, Alex Sangster, interviewed and photographed more than a hundred girl activists in thirteen countries. One led a sting operation against a sex trafficking ring from Dubai. Another group ended single-use plastic bags in Bali, which grew into a global movement inspiring change in over fifty locations. Paola and Alex published *Wonder Girls: Changing Our World* to share what they learned from all of these girls and to invite readers to join their changemaking efforts.

Paola has documented women's issues and women activists around the world for more than twenty years and says that writing this book gave her a new perspective on what girls are capable of—including her own granddaughter. Alex, who also organized a long-running children's program with her sister at a global poverty conference in Mexico when she was eight, says she got a new perspective on her grandmother from the experience. Paola's latest book is *COOL: Women Leaders Reversing Global Warming*, which she developed with Alex's younger sister, Avery, to show the way to a sustainable future.

"

This is not really a story about girls changing the future. This is a story about girls making change today.

"

PAOLA AND ALEX'S STORY

PAOLA: "I had worked in sixty-two different countries, documenting the lives of women and girls. This was book six for me. I had begun to see there were groups of activist girls who were accomplishing astonishing things, and as far as I knew no one had written about that yet. Alex's mom suggested that I consider including Alex in this project. I thought this was a great idea because all of the girls I wanted to invite to participate were between the ages of ten and eighteen. I am seventy-eight. I thought the project would benefit by having someone close to the girls' ages."

ALEX: "Before we started working on this book, my grandmother and I would string beads on bracelets and necklaces and make paper dresses for paper dolls. My sister and I only knew the fun side of my grandmother, the side where she is always laughing and trying to engage us. It's not like she doesn't still do that. But I learned the other side of her, where she also cares about the issues that girls face. This project has offered us opportunities to do things together we would otherwise never have had a chance to do."

PAOLA: "I think the book gave Alex a broader view of the world, and the book gave me a huge respect for Alex. I knew I could always count on her for ideas. She's a very creative photographer. I gave her her first camera when she was about two—when she was so short, she photographed people's feet and the dog's tail. Since she hasn't had lots of photography classes, she's very free about composition. It was liberating for me to do photography with her. She also designed wonderful graphics that we use when we're presenting. She taught me unbelievable amounts about technology and certainly taught me to recognize how little I knew about it. As a result, I have grown more than you can imagine in my respect for her."

ALEX: "My parents sheltered me from a lot of these issues, so before this book I had absolutely no clue what girls are facing. I might have heard of some of these issues, thought about them briefly, and then just gone back to my normal day. But now that I've met the people who face these issues every day and have made personal connections, my perspective has definitely changed. I want to do everything in my power to help their causes. I can't exactly buy them a house, but I can sign a petition. I can donate time. And I can bring awareness of their needs to other people with more resources."

TOOLS TO CHANGE THE WORLD

Share the work

PAOLA: "Alex and I focused on different things when we were doing our research. I focused on the issues and the activism the girls were participating in. Alex focused specifically on what the girls needed and wanted, the barriers they faced, and what readers of the book and the girls in their lives could do to help them. That meant we were putting our attention in different areas of the work."

Build on what you have in common

ALEX: "I got much different responses than my grandmother, and sometimes the girls would elaborate on their lives with me. They were more comfortable talking to me because I'm closer to their ages. I tried my best to include their voices in the sections I wrote because their voices are what need to be heard."

Start today

PAOLA: "Many grown-ups think that girls are the future, but the fact is that girls who are making change have a huge effect on the world right now. Half the girls in Malawi were being married before they were eighteen; most before they were fifteen. There is now a law in place thanks to the girls and their allies. That really has changed the present for them. So this is not really a story about girls changing the future. This is a story about girls making change today."

Take charge and invite others to help

PAOLA: "These girls are doing amazing things literally all by themselves. For example, one started a library in the slum. She knew there wasn't one and that nobody could afford to buy schoolbooks for their children. These girls have the capacity to cause enormous change, often without parents but often with some adult supervision if they need it, and adult expertise when they ask."

Identify opportunities to come together

ALEX: "At an anti-poverty conference in Mexico my grandmother and my dad attended, my sister and I were like, 'But what about the kids? Isn't there something that the kids do?' And there wasn't. So we started an annual gathering of kids from all over the world to develop relationships for when they do start companies or nonprofit organizations to fix a problem in their community."

"

[My father] taught me how closely connected we all are and how important it is that we pay attention to each other.

"

ADVICE TO KEEP GOING

PAOLA: "My father came from Italy to the United States. And I grew up very aware of being part of a global world even at a time when it wasn't nearly as small as it is now, thanks to technology and communications. My father was a doctor committed to making other people more healthy. His example taught me how closely connected we all are and how important it is that we pay attention to each other. It really set the stage for my whole life and my commitment to doing exactly that."

ALEX: "When I was in Guadalajara, Mexico, doing interviews, one of the participants told me, 'We are little particles that can cause change, like the butterfly wings that can create a tsunami in another place.' For me that really puts into perspective that we can all create change no matter what."

BETTY REID SOSKIN

SHARE YOUR HISTORY

When we share our personal stories and speak our truth, we empower the next generation. Betty Reid Soskin says she is inspired to this day by the stories she heard from her great-grandmother Leontine Breaux Allen, a slave from Louisiana who became a midwife and lived until she was 102 and Betty was 27.

Betty is a mother, grandmother, and great-grandmother; a writer and historian; a composer and singer; a social and political activist; and an entrepreneur. She opened one of the first Black-owned record stores in the Bay Area and was a field representative for two California State assemblywomen. She wrote a book, *Sign My Name to Freedom: A Memoir of a Pioneering Life*, and has given talks all over the country about our changing society and Black lives. Betty was instrumental in steering the development of the Rosie the Riveter World War II Home Front National Historical Park in Richmond, California, where she became a park ranger at eighty-five. When she retired in 2021, she was the oldest serving career park ranger in the United States at 100 years old, and still giving weekly talks at the park.

BETTY'S STORY

"As a field representative, the park was created in my assembly district. The Rosie Memorial, which had caught national attention, was less than a mile from my office in Richmond. Even though it was only a mile away, I had never seen fit to visit it because that was a white woman's story. The women in my family had been working outside their homes since slavery. Back in 1942, it had always taken two wages to support Black families. So it wasn't that I was boycotting the Rosie story. It simply had nothing to say to me.

But when the department planners gathered and held their first meetings to frame this [new National Historical] Park as being defined by scattered sites throughout the city, I instantly recognized them as sites of racial segregation. Nobody in that room knew this but me because what gets remembered is determined by who's in the room doing the remembering. There wasn't any grand conspiracy to leave my history out; there simply wasn't anybody in that room that had any reason to know that but me. And I became involved in the planning of the stories.

For example, the Maritime Child Development Center did not service Black families at all. Addison Village was built by the Maritime Commission to temporarily house Kaiser management, but there wouldn't have been any Black managers at the time. Nystrom Village, which was to be restored to show how workers lived, was built by HUD, but you couldn't live in Nystrom Village unless you were white. There wasn't anybody in the room that knew this but me. And while the story of Rosie the Riveter is extremely important as a feminist story and as a feminist icon, there were many, many stories on the home front.

I came on to the National Park Service at first as a consultant on a four-year contract, and after four years became a national park ranger at the age of eighty-five. The congratulations go to the National Park Service. I can't imagine the conversations that were held in Washington about me."

TOOLS TO CHANGE THE WORLD

Set the stage for the next generation

"At my age I have lost my sense of the future. There are no models for me anymore. I've outlived my peer group. What's happened in compensation is that I now am more aware of the past, and I am aware that these periods of chaos are cyclical. I sense we're on an upward spiral. We keep touching the same places at higher and higher levels. I'm not enslaved like my great-grandmother was. Each time we hit one of these places, and we're in one of them now, that's when democracy is being redefined. We have access to the reset button. We're setting the stage for the next generation. And that gives me great hope."

Follow women leaders

"There is so much happening in the women's world right this minute—I would love to be able to say I'm going to be here in order to take advantage of it. Women are cutting new paths. As a woman of color, I think we're finding our places in leadership for the very first time in history. The political structure in the South is being guided by Black women. This is an amazing time to be alive, to be a woman of color."

Keep working on democracy

"It's a fallacy to believe that democracy will ever be fixed. It's a process, and it has to be regenerated by every single generation. It has to be re-created. We'll always be forming that more perfect union. I don't know that we'll ever get there. I'm not sure that's the object."

Look back to move forward

"We have a constitutionally protected right to be wrong, a constitutionally protected right to be bigots if that's what we want to be. But we've also created this incredible National Park System, where it's now possible for us to visit almost any era in our history, the heroic places, the contemplative places, the scenic wonders, the shameful places, and the painful places in order to own that history. Own it, that we may process it in order to begin to forgive ourselves and move toward a more compassionate future."

Value questions more than answers

"If the world could learn to value the questions more than the answers, that would take us a long way. Because it's the questions that lead us to the next questions, which dictates progress."

ADVICE TO KEEP GOING

"I lived my entire life in a constant state of surprise, and I've enjoyed that. I think that I reinvented myself about every ten years. I get restless and I wonder what's coming next. I don't spend much time regretting yesterday nor planning for tomorrow. It's all now for me. I think I'm using everything I've ever learned right now. Right now all of the women that I ever was are here in me. They are triggered by a song or a story or something I run into as I'm going through the laundry. And being that complex woman at this point in my life is so exciting in itself, I don't know that I would wish for anything more than what's going on right this minute."

"

I'm using everything I've
ever learned right now.
All of the women
that I ever was
are here in me.

"

WHO'S IN THIS BOOK

ANNA LAPPÉ (PAGE 43)

realfoodmedia.org

Best-selling author and advocate for justice and sustainability across the food chain

ANNE-MARIE SLAUGHTER (PAGE 142)

newamerica.org/our-people

Patriot, entrepreneur, mother, mentor, thinker, feminist, CEO of New America

A'SHANTI GHOLAR (PAGE 147)

lnk.bio/ashantigholar

President of Emerge, founder of The Brown Girls Guide to Politics, womxnist

BETTY REID SOSKIN (PAGE 187)

soapboxinc.com/betty-reid-soskin

Park ranger, storyteller, antiwar and civil rights activist, and jazz musician

CAROLINE PAUL (PAGE 75)

carolinepaul.com

New York Times best-selling author of six books for both adults and kids

CARRIE GOLDBERG (PAGE 175)

cagoldberglaw.com

Founding attorney at victims' rights law firm C. A. Goldberg, PLLC, and author

EMILY LADAU (PAGE 161)

emilyladau.com

Disability rights activist and author

EVE RODSKY (PAGE 33)

fairplaylife.com

Author, attorney, and activist; founder of the Fair Play Policy Institute; cofounder of The Careforce

FAVIANNA RODRIGUEZ (PAGE 16)

favianna.com

Interdisciplinary artist, cultural organizer, and social justice activist

GLORIA STEINEM (PAGE 113)

gloriasteinem.com

Writer, lecturer, political activist, and feminist organizer

HEATHER McTEER TONEY (PAGE 103)

heathermcteertoney.com

Author, community advocate, climate and environmental expert; mother of free Black children, life partner, source of wisdom, kindness, and sass; planet protector

IJEOMA OLUO (PAGE 61)

ijeomaoluo.com

Writer, speaker, and internet yeller; *New York Times* best-selling author

ILYSE HOGUE (PAGE 91)

purpose.com

Author, changer of systems, driver of social impact

ISHA CLARKE (PAGE 21)

youthvsapocalypse.org

Cofounder of Youth vs. Apocalypse

JOAN BLADES (PAGE 156)

livingroomconversations.org
momsrising.org

Cofounder of Living Room Conversations, MoveOn, and MomsRising; domestic peace builder, mediator, entrepreneur, and movement organizer

KATE SCHATZ (PAGE 26)

kateschatz.com

New York Times best-selling author, activist, public speaker, and queer feminist mama

LILY TOMLIN (PAGE 37)

Actress, comedian, writer, singer, and producer

MARGARITA QUIHUIS (PAGE 86)

margaritaquihuis.com
peaceinnovation.com

CEO, Peace Institute at The Hague; Executive Director, Peace Innovation Lab at Stanford; Founding Director, Astia

MIRIAM KLEIN STAHL (PAGE 26)

miriamkleinstahl.com

New York Times best-selling illustrator; cofounder of the Arts and Humanities Academy at Berkeley High School; public artist, activist, and parent

PAOLA GIANTURCO AND ALEX SANGSTER (PAGE 181)

paolagianturcoauthor.com

Paola is author/photographer of seven books about women activists around the world; her granddaughter Alex was coauthor of *Wonder Girls: Changing Our World*

RACHEL SIMMONS (PAGE 168)

rachelsimmons.com

Author, cofounder of Girls Leadership, and educator

REBECCA TRAISTER (PAGE 68)

Author of *Good and Mad: The Revolutionary Power of Women's Anger*

RESHMA SAUJANI (PAGE 132)

reshmasaujani.com

Founder of Girls Who Code and Marshall Plan for Moms, and author

RHEA SUH (PAGE 56)

marincf.org/about/mcf-leadership

President and CEO of Marin Community Foundation

SARAH McBRIDE (PAGE 127)

sarahmcbride.com

Activist and politician

SARAH SILVERMAN (PAGE 109)

twitter.com/SarahKSilverman

Two-time Emmy Award–winning comedian, actress, writer, and producer

SEANE CORN (PAGE 51)

seanecorn.com

International yoga teacher, author, public speaker, and cofounder of Off the Mat, Into the World

SHANNON WATTS (PAGE 137)

momsdemandaction.org
fightlikeamother.org

Founder of Moms Demand Action for Gun Sense in America and author

TERESA YOUNGER (PAGE 121)

forwomen.org

Activist, advocate, renowned public speaker, organizational strategist, and proven leader in the philanthropic and policy sectors, president and CEO of Ms. Foundation for Women

THE KITCHEN SISTERS: DAVIA NELSON AND NIKKI SILVA (PAGE 97)

kitchensisters.org

Peabody, duPont-Columbia, and James Beard Award–winning radio producers, podcasters, journalists, storytellers, collaborators, and authors

TIFFANY SHLAIN (PAGE 79)

tiffanyshlain.com

Artist, Emmy-nominated filmmaker, founder of the Webby Awards, best-selling author and public speaker

ACKNOWLEDGMENTS

Deep thanks from Lauren and Hadley to:

Our wonderful partners in bringing this book into the world—Rosy Petri, for your creative vision and collaboration; our agent, Laura Mazer, for your guidance and ceaseless energy; Isabel McCarthy, Allison Chi, and the entire team at Countryman Press for believing in the possibilities.

The many, many people who read, commented, listened, advised, and cheered us on as we shaped this book into being. Special shout-outs to Craig Bankey, Dana Smith, Etienne Lehrer, Eve Rodsky, Gabrielle Tenaglia, Hillary Goidell, Jenny Summers, Jenny Wapner, Jennifer Werner, Kate Schatz, Kate and Scott McGlashan, Laura Counts, Lisa Coris, Liz Morgan, Maya Dillard Smith, MJ "Bo" Bogatin, Michael Mechanic, Paige Steinman, Rozella Kennedy, Ruth Whippman, Sarah and Don Moore, Sharon Backurz, and Tiffany Shlain. Danielle Cass, for introducing us in the first place.

The biggest of thanks to the thirty leaders whose stories, tools, and advice we included here; every guest on *Inflection Point* who informed our thinking and this book; and to you, our readers and listeners.

Special thanks from Lauren to:

My unwaveringly supportive extended family; my husband, for being my sounding board and nourishing my creative spirit; my mom, who inspires me; my little brother, who gives the best advice; my stepfather, for always being interested; and my dad, who always said, "just ask," and who I miss every day. For my brilliant, strong daughters, I love you always.

Hadley, for your friendship, your partnership, and going on this adventure with me. You have given me the greatest gift—your time.

While most of my conversations took place in the KALW studio, some took place onstage. Several have been excerpted here. Thanks to the teams at The Commonwealth Club of San Francisco, starting with Marissa Levine and George Dobbins; the Bay Area Book Festival/

Women Lit, Cherilyn Parsons, Scott Gelfand, Samee Roberts; Bioneers, Nina Simons and Stephanie Welch.

Inflection Point would not be the same without: KALW, Matt Martin, Eric Wayne, and Ashleyanne Krigbaum; Alaura Weaver; PRX, the Corporation for Public Broadcasting, and Project Catapult, in particular John Barth, Kerri Hoffman, and Enrico Benjamin, "feedback is a gift." Liz Scarboro and Kelsey Crowe for generous introductions at key points in this journey. Sabrina Moyle, Ruth Ann Harnisch and Jenny Raymond, and all our supporters.

My fellow travelling campers, where to next?

Special thanks from Hadley to:

My husband, Kent, for always going along with my time-intensive, world-changing, life projects. My parents, for showing me what it's like to take risks and make things happen. And my two incredible daughters, for giving me perspective and purpose.

Lauren, for believing in me and for our partnership and the potential for these stories to help change the world. My Aunt Sharon, for mailing me Julia Cameron's *The Artist's Way* so many years ago. The Ladiez in my life who keep me going with advice, help, and moral support. And the many, many others who give me energy, share in my joy and disappointments, and provide sustenance when I need it (even when I think I don't . . . because I always do).

Photo credits to:

Bobby Gordon	Ijeoma Oluo	Norman Seef
Casey Orr	Isha Clarke	Olga Shmaidenko
Chris Langford with Chris Langford Photography	Jacquelyn Warner	Paige Green
	Jennifer Werner	Robyn Von Swank
Everett Collection Inc / Alamy Stock Photo	Jenny Risher	Scott Sangster
	Jock McDonald	Victoria Stevens
	Julia Zave	

ABOUT THE AUTHORS AND ILLUSTRATOR

Lauren Schiller is an award-winning interviewer and the creator of numerous podcasts and radio shows. Both in studio and live on stage, she hosts in-depth conversations that elicit surprising stories and reveal insightful truths about the world we live in, how we got here, and where we go next. She and her husband have two daughters who show them what's possible every day. Listen to her interviews at inflectionpointradio.org

Hadley Dynak is an activist, nonprofit leader, and creative producer. She works to raise the visibility of social issues and causes, connect people with changemaking opportunities, and drive local action. Her two daughters inspire her to make the world better, every day. She and her husband split time between the Bay Area and Sonoma County in California, where they own a historic public garden.

Rosy Petri fuses portraiture and storytelling as an act of witness. She's been an Artist-in-Residence at the bell hooks center and Pfister Hotel, a Nohl Emerging Artist Fellow, and Mildred Harpole Artist of the Year. Her art and fine craft can be found at www.thisisparadisehome.com.

"

Trust in your power to change the world.

"